Your Child Can Think Like A Genius

Your Child Can Think Like a Genius

How to Unlock the Gifts in Every Child

Bernadette Tynan

thorsons

Thorsons
An Imprint of HarperCollins*Publishers*
77–85 Fulham Palace Road
Hammersmith, London W6 8JB

The website address is:
www.thorsonselement.com

and *Thorsons* are trademarks of
HarperCollins*Publishers* Ltd

First published 2004

1 3 5 7 9 10 8 6 4 2

A catalogue record for this book is
available from the British Library

ISBN 0 00 716073 9

Cartoons by Harry Venning

Printed and bound in Great Britain by
Martins the Printers Ltd, Berwick Upon Tweed

Contents

Activities

For all the parents who work hard every day,
love their children, cherish their happiness
and want only the best for them.
Wherever you are in the world, this book
is dedicated to you and your children.

acknowledgments

It takes a great many people to get any book to press and this book has been no exception. My thanks go first to Wanda Whiteley at Thorsons Element, for her sharp intellect and vision, Barbara Wolff at the Albert Einstein Archives, Jackie Newman for her dedication unto the last whilst also being eight months pregnant, Matthew Cory for his patience, wisdom and wit, all the team I met and didn't get to meet at Thorsons Element, Simon Gerratt, Kate Latham, Susanna Abbott, Natasha Tait, Jacqui Caulton and illustrator Harry Venning. Thank you all and one.

The support of family and friends cannot be measured. Thank you doesn't really say it, but I am going to say it anyway. Thank you to my parents Chris and Pat, my family: Bob and Kaye, my self-styled 'international sister' Alice Amy, Chris and James. My friends: Asraf and Saida, Fazeela, Cristen and Danny and their son Alistair, Sarah and Darren, Helen and Simon and their daughter Rosie, Peter, Marion, Ellen and John, – thank you for your support and friendship throughout. And finally I would like to say thank you to my dog Beth, for listening intently, saying nothing, and being especially gifted at sharing biscuits during tea breaks.

The little girl had the making of a poet in her who, being told to be sure of her meaning before she spoke, said: 'How can I know what I think till I see what I say?'

THE ART OF THOUGHT

Introduction

What every parent and child should know

What if you could show your child how to discover, unlock and develop their natural gifts and creativity? You hold in your hands a book that shows you how to do exactly that. Every child's gifts are as individual as their own thumb print. And every parent has the right to know how they can best help their children develop their special gifts and talents. This book has been written therefore especially for you. Underpinning it is the belief that *all* children, wherever they are in the world, should be able to have the advantage of knowing how to tap into, and develop their own natural gifts and talents – *today*.

Essential knowledge and skills for life – whatever their age

Whether your child is just starting junior school or is in the final stages of their school career, they have here a treasure trove of knowledge to help them think, learn and succeed. Grounded in both research and practical experience of working with individual children and parents, this book equips children with the knowledge and skills to become masters of their own learning – whatever their age. They will learn how to develop:

★ individual gifts and talents;
★ an effective and flexible learning strategy that works for *them*;
★ independent thinking skills;
★ their own creativity.

Thinking like a genius

Have you ever wondered how an Einstein, da Vinci or Mozart thought so creatively, learned their subjects so well, and developed their talents to such a level? I certainly have. When I started my research, the first thing I noticed about the lives of past geniuses was that having opportunities to be creative and express their individual ideas had been an important factor in their development from childhood. Today children's school experience is punctuated by tests for basic skills and for just about everything else. Statistical measurements are used widely to gauge our children's abilities. I wondered what past geniuses might make of all this if they were around today. What if the way we were learning had become so basic-skills focused, so test oriented that if, say, Mozart was in junior school he may be not only bored, but highly frustrated with test after test, because it was as if his individual gifts, thinking and creativity were being hemmed in at every step? Pondering this question, I realized that a child need not be Mozart to feel the same way.

New era, new focus

The advent of the global knowledge economy has highlighted the importance of individual ideas, creativity, independent thinking and even intellectual property. But none of these 21st century 'facts of life' sit well with traditional mass education systems the roots of which lie in the 19th century. This has forced a rethink to begin in education systems world-wide. With all the pressures of our fast paced lives you may have been too busy to notice this. But right now your child is in the middle of some of the biggest changes in education since the industrial revolution.

So what is happening and why? Traditionally mass education systems were designed to prepare children to store facts, gather knowledge and reproduce it in examinations. Jobs and careers were for life. Today, economies are more volatile, careers more likely to change. Our children can expect to have a range of careers as new markets and technologies emerge, and with it new opportunities are created. At the same time, the speed of communications technology means that new knowledge is being produced rapidly all the time. The ability therefore not just to learn, but learn rapidly, and view learning as a life-long process rather than a one-stop shop, becomes emphasised. Again, I wondered what Mozart, Einstein or da Vinci would feel about all of this. How might they feel as a child at school, aware of the rapidly changing world around them, doing their tests year after year, looking outside their classroom window wondering what they would do when they left school?

One size doesn't fit all in learning

All of this got me thinking about how we are taught to learn when we are at school. In the last century there was an explosion of learning theories for children. All of these theories focused, as did mass education systems, upon teaching children knowledge learning, as opposed to knowledge *creation*. Being able to show that we can learn knowledge, via examinations, is of course an important skill in life, but then in the global knowledge economy of the 21st century as we have seen above, so is being able to express our ideas, *create* knowledge, learn quickly and develop individual gifts and creativity as best we can. The challenges of combining learning with creativity may be new to this century, but not to past geniuses: their lives show that their success lay in their ability to learn and create all at the same time.

I started to search for a theory of learning that could help children today, do what geniuses had always done. Working with a wide range of children, parents and schools from different parts of the world, I realized that no matter how well thought through, or well-meaning any learning theories are, in the end they are just theories. In practice, 'one size doesn't (and cannot) fit all'. When you think about it, why should it be any other way? From the clothes we wear, to the food we eat and the medicines that we take, the last few years have seen people everywhere re-affirming a fact that has become lost since the advent of mass produced goods – each one of us is totally unique. Learning is no different. Education systems may be mass produced but each of our children is an original. And when it comes to genius if there is one factor that unites them all it is their hallmark: individuality. Mozart, da Vinci and Einstein *did it their way*. They believed in their own gifts and had the confidence to pursue them in the way they thought best.

The more I considered all these factors together, the more I searched for a system of learning that would help our children really maximize on their natural gifts and equip them for life and learning in the 21st century. *I found none!* In a way that made me angry because I felt that in an age that made such a fuss of each new technological invention, we had missed out on the best bit of technology ever – our children's gifts and natural creativity. We owe it to our children to give them a system of learning that sets them free to think like a genius, develop their individual gifts, and thumb print their learning to suit *them* best. That is what is set out in these pages.

Thumb Print Learning® is not another prescriptive, 'one size fits all' theory. It is an opportunity for children to discover their own gifts and talents and take charge of their own learning for *their* future. It gives *them* the knowledge about how they think and learn, so that they can create their own system of learning that is as unique to them as their thumb print – because it works for *them*.

Designed with the busy parent in mind

None of us has enough time and this book has been written with that fact very much in mind. You have probably always had questions that you have wanted to ask about your child's individual gifts, creativity, thinking and learning, but either you never had the time, or there was no expert to hand to answer them. The structure provides all the information you need therefore in a quick and easy reference format.

Frequently asked questions

As you go through these chapters, you will find that no stone has been left unturned in answering the most frequent questions I get asked by parents. Throughout, FAQ sections provide an added source of information, and if you want to pursue a particular topic of interest to you, a list of useful website addresses is provided for you in the 'Where can I get information on …?' section.

Brainboxes

Want to become an instant expert on something quickly? Got a burning question that you would like answered before you tackle an imminent parent's evening? Help is at hand! Brainboxes at the end of each chapter summarize all the main points about topics so that you can dip in and out and find out what you want, where you want, when you want.

Fun activities for your child

Fun learning is smart learning. Flick through this book and you will find that it is packed with enjoyable and ready-to-use activities to help children unlock their individual gifts and creativity and develop their thinking and learning skills.

Your child's gifts

Section I explodes all the age-old myths about genius to reveal the fact that the individual ability of *every* child is limitless. Section II shows you how to discover your child's gifts. Ability tests are unravelled, to give you the inside track on how they actually work, and what they can *really* tell you about your child's gifts.

Top tips are given on how to work with schools to help your child develop their natural abilities, and which signs and symptoms to look out for to ensure that your child is being appropriately challenged (in other words, that they are not bored!) at school. Sections III and IV are packed full of activities to help children discover and develop their own natural gifts for themselves. Right now though, there is probably just one question on your mind. Can my child *really* learn how to think like a genius? The short answer is 'yes', chapter 1 explains why.

section one

Genius – Exploding the Myths

Chapter 1

Genius: Born or Made?

If ever there was a subject steeped in myth, this is it. Mention the word 'genius' and the images most likely to spring to mind are either of an ancient, white-haired scientist dabbling with calculus, or a child with 'X-file' qualities who frightens everyone witless with their abilities at the ripe old age of three. Hollywood has a lot to answer for! But if we cut through the myths, what facts are we actually left with? Get your trainers on! In this chapter we are going for a quick brain jog. In a few minutes from now you will be an expert on this topic.

FAQ

 Q: Isn't it all genetic?

 A: Whenever I give a seminar, this question is guaranteed to get everyone going when it comes up. Is it nature or is it nurture that predicts our future? For the record, all the current indications are that it is just too simple to say we are born with what we get and that is that. Thinking that the genetic cards nature dealt us at birth predicts our future, rests entirely on the theory that our brain's intelligence and abilities are fixed at birth. Whereas, the evidence to date strongly suggests that this is not the case. Here are the reasons why.

'Late' versus 'early' bloomers

At the start of the 20th century, psychology was still a relatively new science, but it began to have a greater presence in the debate about human capability. Whereas philosophy had used logic and reasoning to explore the human mind, psychology introduced the idea of testing to try and define and measure people's intelligence. Once people were tested and achieved a score, it was thought that both their score and therefore their intelligence were static over a lifetime. This idea was flawed. In reality, when people were tested at different times in their lives their scores changed. And it isn't just test scores that are subject to change. The fact is people find themselves excelling at different times in their lives. Some people may bloom in their earlier years at school, others later in life. Think back and you probably know someone yourself who flunked school, but did perfectly great after they left. We have all heard of entrepreneurs who dropped out of school and made their first million while their schoolfriends were still slogging it out at university. None of us bloom all at the same time, and it is difficult to put an end point on what anyone is capable of achieving in their lifetime.

Don't let anyone tell you any different – environment counts!

The main problem with the idea that we are a product of our genes and nothing else is that we do not of course develop in a little glass bubble in isolation from the world, impervious to what goes on around us. Although after a bad day at the office, or fighting our way around a supermarket on a Friday night, this idea may sound attractive! As human beings we arrive here with a survival kit, but we grow and develop within a process of constant interaction with our environment.

What would happen to our brain development if we didn't have any social contact from the time we were born? Obviously, for good ethical and humanitarian reasons, legitimate experiments are not carried out to find out what would happen if a baby was left to develop on its own in total isolation. However, sadly, there have been cases where children have been discovered who were raised with severely minimized social interaction. Brain development within these children, including speech and language were radically impaired. Providing children with a nurturing, supportive and socially interactive environment is not just good for their self-esteem, emotional development and overall well-being; it is no less than paramount for their cognitive brain function and intellectual development.

Genes are finite, whereas the potential of our brain is infinite

Environment cannot be ignored in human development for another simple reason which is grounded in the mathematical law of probability. The genes we inherit are *finite*, whereas the brain's ability to develop billions of new connections between the cells it is born with is *infinite*. Education, knowledge, learning and experiences – all of these will greatly influence the number of new connections each of our brains will make over a lifetime.

It's official – the brain never stops growing

OK, so the potential for connections to form between our brain cells are infinite, but we are born with only so many brain cells and we can't make any more, right? Wrong.

Traditionally, the received wisdom has been that we are born with a certain number of brain cells and that is that. We have all been taught that if you do not use your grey cells you lose them. What scientists discovered at the close of the 20th century meant that this cliché now packs an extra punch. It was found that our brain grows new cells or neurons all the time; and as with our existing brain cells, the trick is to stimulate them to prevent them from dying off. This may not seem such a fantastic discovery, but in reality the implications are massive. It changes everything. *What we are born with matters, but what we do with it matters even more*!

FAQ

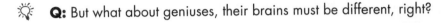 **Q:** But what about geniuses, their brains must be different, right?

A: The first problem with this question is that no one knows what a genius really is, other than the chances of a person being hailed as one is greatly increased by the number of years they have been dead. The second problem is we don't know if there is such a thing as an atypical genius brain. This is because there is a severe shortage of genius brains available for scientists to rummage around in. This brings us back to the first problem. A genius has to be dead before scientists can rummage around inside their brains – you see the problem.

Einstein kindly left his brain to science, and given the aforementioned shortage, it has done star-ship mileage around the globe ever since. One of the most striking things about Einstein's brain is its robust network of connectivity in comparison with the brains of other people his age. Put another way, his brain seems to have been particularly well wired up.

However, and this is a *big* however, whether Einstein's brain was born like this, or whether it developed to become like this over time, via his interaction with his environment, a life dedicated to research and learning, is something that cannot be known for certain. This is because, of course, we don't know what his brain looked like inside when he was first born.

Neuroscience is the relatively new kid on the block in brain study. The favoured method of studying the brain in neuroscience is brain imaging. Using this technique we can monitor which parts of the brain children use when they encounter different problem-solving situations. For example, we can monitor the brain activity of a child who is good at mathematics in comparison with a child who is less able in mathematics, to see how their brains tackle the problem as they work through it. You may have seen pictures of brain images like this in the media from time to time. But what are these images really able to tell us about brains?

Looking at the brain like this is a bit like taking aerial photographs of weather systems. But, as we all know, looking at a stormy weather front on an aerial picture is not the same as being the poor soul caught in the downpour at the ground level. In other words, looking at brain scans and images, no matter how sophisticated they may be, at present tell us more about the hardware than the finer workings of the inner software of the brain. In short they do not reveal whether people's brains on the *inside* are any different from one individual to another.

Even if, magically, a safe way was found to take a look inside a baby's brain at birth to see whether or not it looked like Einstein's older brain, for all the reasons discussed earlier, this would not determine genius. Plus – and here's the real kicker – Einstein did not consider himself to be a genius at all. As you and your child will discover in the activities later in this book, Einstein had his own ideas about his abilities and how he came to develop them.

So what *do* we know for certain? When you take away all the hype and mystique surrounding genius, one simple fact remains: all recorded geniuses began their journey in the world just like any other baby. They arrived safe and warm with a brain and a body hungry for development. After that, as with all babies, they found themselves in an environment and what happened next mattered. The following analogy demonstrates why.

Getting to be a 'tall plant' takes nurture as well as nature

In 1984, the biologist Lewontin pointed out that if you take two equally well-formed plant seedlings, and then you put one of these seedlings in a nutrient-rich environment, the plant grows tall and blooms wonderfully. If you take the other equally well-formed plant seedling and put it in a nutrient-deficient environment, plant growth is stunted. Environment, not the biological inheritance of these seedlings has determined their actual growth and success in each case. In gardening terms then, now you know: this book is all about providing your child with some excellent 'nutrients' to help their natural gifts blossom. Getting to be a 'tall plant' takes nurture as well as nature.

Does this analogy bear any relationship to the childhood experiences of history's geniuses?

Learning from the childhoods of Mozart, da Vinci and Einstein

Mozart's father was an established court violinist and musician in Salzburg, Austria. He coached his son in the harpsichord, violin and music whilst Mozart was still in his early years. The child Mozart enjoyed fame quickly; his father was able to introduce him to circles of influential people, using his position as a court musician in Salzburg. Age was not seen as a barrier to Mozart being able to learn and develop complex musical technique. When the young Mozart showed his interest in music above all other things, his parents encouraged him and supported him in this absolutely.

From a small child, Leonardo da Vinci's parents supported him in his enthusiasm to explore very wide-ranging interests including mathematics, science, music and art. In his early teens, da Vinci became an apprentice at the studio of an established and respected artist of the day, Andrea del Verrocchio. During his time at del Verrocchio's studio, da Vinci developed his artistic skills. At the same time, however, he was still able to carry on his talent for scientific inventions, using his artistic ability to depict his revolutionary ideas with great visual detail and clarity.

In contrast, Einstein's early years were more in line with today's conventional educational experience. From being a baby, his family supported him greatly in developing his gifts and talents. He started his school career with primary school and ended it in higher education. Contrary to popular myth, Einstein was not a man obsessed with science, his interests both in his childhood and later life were always more diverse than that. In his youth he explored religious thought and ethics, and took up the violin when he was 12 – something which he continued throughout his life. His parents allowed him to take his entrance examinations to higher education at the age of 16, two years younger than was ordinarily the case. Unfortunately, Einstein failed the entrance test. Undeterred, he stayed on at school and entered higher education at the Federal Polytechnic Institute in Zurich a year later. However, it was not during his formal education that Einstein's gifts really blossomed and came into their own. Compared to da Vinci and Mozart, Einstein was a late bloomer. It was to be eight years later, after his graduation from the Federal Polytechnic Institute, and working in a number of different jobs, including those of temporary schoolteacher and patents clerk, that his thinking, ideas and creativity began to be discovered and recognized by the wider world via academia. The rest is history.

FAQ

 Q: Were Mozart, Da Vinci and Einstein all born into rich families?

 A: Whenever I get asked this in seminars my answer is always the same: it depends what you mean by rich. If you mean families rich in their support of their children's gifts the answer is 'yes'. If you mean families rich in the economic sense the answer is that neither Mozart's, da Vinci's nor Einstein's family were especially wealthy.

So, what do all three childhoods of these geniuses have in common?

The foundations of genius

♦ Parents who believed in their abilities as children and supported them;
♦ Individual abilities in various fields;
♦ Opportunities to develop their own individual gifts and talents;
♦ No sense of any limits being set on their abilities;
♦ Age immaterial, ability the focus;
♦ Discovery, recognition and appreciation of their abilities by others.

If you unpack these key points, there are a lot of 'what ifs' associated with becoming recognized as a genius. What if Leonardo da Vinci's parents had not been supportive of their child's enthusiasm to explore his interests in such a diverse range of subject areas? What if academia had not appreciated Einstein's ideas in the end? What if Mozart's father had not encouraged his son's enthusiasm for music and had forced him to do something else instead? Whatever else their individual gifts may have been, without being discovered, recognized and appreciated by others, starting with their own family, history may never have come to know them as 'geniuses'. There is another question here: what if they hadn't been born where they were, when they were?

What if Einstein had been an Eskimo?

Genius – being in the right place at the right time?

What if Einstein had been an Eskimo? Let's imagine for a moment that Einstein had not been born in Central Europe. Instead, he was born the son of an Eskimo living in a remote region of Greenland. Being a young son of an Eskimo in the 19th century would not have reduced his ability to be a genius, but being isolated from the rest of the world, and speaking a language that few in Europe could understand, would certainly have limited his chances of being discovered.

Historically being male and European seems to have helped tremendously in being crowned a genius. Hence three names dominate popular culture in the genius stakes. Whether we are in Singapore, London or Toronto mention the word 'genius' and up pop Mozart, da Vinci and Einstein. When each of these three geniuses was around, being fluent in specifically European languages, alongside being a male, gave the would-be genius distinct advantages: they could get their ideas heard and their talents discovered. In short, if you could not access these advantages you had little chance of going down in history as a genius.

It is a sombre thought when you think about it. It is probable that there have been millions of people from all the world's different races, creeds and cultures whose brilliant ideas have been lost to human history, *just because they were not fluent in a particular language at any given time*, and were therefore prevented from having their ideas and talents being discovered.

Being stumped by not speaking or writing the 'right' language at the right time, is just one way potential geniuses could have been snuffed out in bygone times. Until recently being a woman was another. Unless a woman inherited, or acquired by marriage, a position of power and influence, or was lucky enough to have had a forward-thinking father or spouse, trying to prove they were a genius at anything other than knitting was, well, difficult! Although not quickly enough, things have since moved on and, in the 20th century, females finally began to get a taste of the public recognition and respect accorded their male counterparts for their innovation and ideas. Consider the famous story of Hedy Lamarr and it is easy to see how would-be geniuses don't always get it right, simply because they are in the wrong place at the wrong time.

A woman not of her time

If you have ever found yourself watching a 1940s movie, you will have seen Hedy Lamarr, even if you didn't know who she was. One of her most famous roles was as the beautiful seductress Delilah in *Samson and Delilah*. But that is not the remarkable thing about her at all. Yes, she was an extremely beautiful and successful actress, but these weren't her only gifts. During the Second World War she came up with a system for alternating frequencies so that radio messages between the allies could be sent without the enemy being able to intercept them. Her idea was brilliant and successful. It is alleged that she wanted to use her talent for invention to develop more ideas to help the war effort, but was advised that she would serve the American people better by focusing upon her acting career. Consequently her genius for invention only became public knowledge toward the end of her life in the late 1990s. When, as an old lady, Lamarr was told that she had finally been awarded the recognition she was due for her genius, it is rumoured that she said simply: 'About time!'

Hedy Lamarr had a fabulous idea, but being a glamorous Hollywood actress was a mixed blessing for her. Had she been around today she may have pursued a very different road to fame and fortune. She was a person who was just *ahead* of her time. In the end, however, Lamarr was one of the luckier ones. At least she was recognized – *eventually*. But what about all the people who were never recognized for the abilities they had to offer? What happened to them? We will of course never know the answer to that.

The 21st century – renaissance of genius?

The good news is that unlike children in the past, your child has an unprecedented opportunity afforded by 21st-century communications technology – the opportunity to have their individual ideas and creativity communicated *globally*. The internet is by no means perfect, but one thing it does do is to shrink the world down so that it does not matter who you are or where you are from, it is your ideas that count. Whether you are a man or a woman, 18 or 75, live in Iceland or Venezuela you can have your ideas heard and discovered.

At the same time, communications technology provides an unprecedented potential for the sharing of ideas, and this in itself may lead to a renaissance in genius in this century. What do I mean? Imagine if Leonardo da Vinci, Einstein, Hedy Lamarr and Mozart had all been alive today and had e-mail! What ideas and inventions might the world be benefiting from now? Alternatively, view this scenario another way. Replace these famous names of history with the live and kicking children of today and the potential of new communications technology to reveal tomorrow's geniuses becomes more real.

The achievements of past geniuses may have been great, but perhaps we have not seen anything yet. Who knows, they could just have been a tiny glimpse of the range and diversity of talent, gifts and creativity that the world's children have to offer. Your child has been born at the right time and in the right place!

No one is a genius 'til I say so!

You may have read through the second part of this chapter and thought to yourself: '*Yeah, right, but no one would have rejected Einstein's ideas because they were revolutionary*' or '*Everyone knew that Leonardo da Vinci was a genius because his work was so brilliant*'. But remember, without someone somewhere formally recognizing that they had something to offer, even the big three names of genius were going nowhere fast with their ideas. One of the greatest myths of all about genius is that they are born, everyone instantly recognizes them as a genius, that is that and the rest is history. Before I came to research the history of genius no one was more adamant than me at arguing that this must be the case. However, as I soon discovered, the concept of genius is more socially constructed than popular myth would have us believe. It takes at least two to become a genius – a person with an idea or gift and someone in their society not only to see it, but *believe* in it, for a genius to happen. And as we saw with all of the big three names in the history of genius, that belief in their gifts and ideas started at home, in their childhoods, with the support of their parents. Nothing has changed in the 21st century. Ever wondered how a Julia Roberts, a David Beckham, a Tiger Woods or Venus and Serena Williams got started? Mum and Dad or a mentor figured highly.

Congratulations, you can take your running shoes off now. You are an expert in genius!

Brainbox

- ① Intelligence isn't fixed from birth.
- ① The genes we inherit are finite; the brain's ability to develop is infinite.
- ① Up until the turn of this century, it was wrongly assumed that the number of brain cells we are born with was static; in reality new brain cells are being born all the time, and to keep them alive we need to stimulate them.
- ① Environment matters to stimulate brain growth. It matters for our children, it mattered for Einstein, da Vinci and Mozart.
- ① All geniuses started off in exactly the same way, they had parents who supported the development of their individual gifts and talents.

- ☉ Einstein did not consider himself to be a genius.
- ☉ History shows that no one is a genius until someone says they are. In this sense it takes two to be a genius: someone with ideas, and someone to discover, recognize and believe in them.
- ☉ In the past not being the right gender, or speaking the 'right' language, at the right time prevented people from having their ideas discovered.
- ☉ The good news is that the unprecedented opportunity afforded by global communications technology for children to have their ideas heard, shared and discovered exists today. This in itself could see a true renaissance of genius in the 21st century. Your child has been born in the right place at the right time. *Now* is the time to have their gifts discovered and developed.

section two

Discovering Your Child's Gifts

Chapter 2

What's in a Test?

Putting tests in perspective: in da Vinci's day there weren't any!

Whenever I am helping parents get inside international ability tests, I find it is always useful to start by first getting tests in perspective. Ability tests haven't always been around. Indeed they didn't exist in da Vinci's day. And from all accounts, he seems to have done perfectly well without them.

Today, mention the word 'test' and parents and children start to break out in a cold sweat, and with good reason. Wherever we find ourselves in the world, our children face a barrage of tests in their education, often starting in their younger years at school. How did this fuss about tests get started? What does all of this mean for our children? And what has happened since da Vinci's day that has put testing at the very heart of children's education, and consequently their development in the 21st century?

One of the key reasons is the advent and proliferation of mass education systems globally. By definition, mass education systems are large organizations. Large organizations need managing and management needs structure. And in this case, structure means imposing an order in which our children learn. Hence, what you learn, and when you learn it, becomes decided by which year group you are in. Then you are left with the question of how you are going to measure what is happening in the system that has been created.

Globally there has been an explosion in the use of statistical measures in mass education systems. Testing provides the perfect statistical data because it is numbers based. Of course, test scores alone don't mean anything unless you have something to correlate them with. Age is the obvious and ideal correlation because it is another number and therefore easily lends itself to statistical analysis. The inevitable result of this is that we all get caught up in a vast number-crunching exercise in which tests become a central focus for schools, because school effectiveness becomes inextricably tied in with performance in test results.

No matter, therefore, how good the intent of mass education systems, an emphasis on regular testing, together with the actual way in which children's learning is structured into age or year groups, achieves two things:

1   Puts tests at the centre of education and learning;
2   Places an artificial age barrier on children's individual abilities.

Within such a system of learning a child unavoidably becomes viewed as exceptional when they can show they can learn material 'beyond their years'. But how accurate is it to claim that ordinarily children's abilities are predicated by age anyway?

Age is not the gatekeeper of ability

The idea that a child's ability to learn is age dependent is a relatively new one in human history. If, for instance, we go back to the Middle Ages we see that age and ability were thought of differently at that time. Elizabeth I, one of the most famous and successful queens in European history was an accomplished philosopher, historian, politician, and multi-lingual – *before* her teens. There is absolutely nothing in research to say that children are not as capable today.

A child doesn't Know that something is complex – until we tell them it is

Who then is best placed to say what a child is or is not capable of understanding or learning at any given age – us, armed with a bunch of education statistics, or them? Any parent who has spent hours trying to sort out their laptop, or struggled all week to stop their digital wrist watch going off every 15 minutes, only to have their five-year-old fix it for them in under 10 seconds, knows exactly what I mean. A child does not know that something is too complex for them until we tell them that it is. If we pre-condition them into thinking their abilities are somehow predicated by their age, then we are putting the brakes on them before they even got started. We are presuming that we know the limits of what they are capable of, and when they will be able to achieve it. Well-meaning or not, in a more scientific way this is exactly what ability tests do. If they were not based on pre-set expectations and markers on ability, what is considered simple or complex, they would not function as tests at all.

This brings us to the other reason, outside of mass educations systems, why testing has become so embedded in our children's learning. Since the likes of Elizabeth I and da Vinci were around, another field of thought has rocketed into human history: psychology.

Testing children's abilities

While, as discussed in Section I, psychology was still a relatively new science at the beginning of the 20th century, today it exerts a huge influence in the way our children's abilities are measured and tested at school. This is fine as long as we are not left blinded by the science and understand exactly what it is that each test is measuring. This chapter is here to help you do that. We are going to start by getting inside that bastion of tests: IQ. It is almost as shrouded in myth and mystique as genius is. So let's get down to some basic facts.

FAQs

Q: Does IQ = ability?

A: No, the specific role of an IQ test is to measure intelligence in some way – this is just one way of trying to quantify and measure a child's abilities.

Q: Are children with high IQs more likely to be academic types?

A: No. People with high IQs may or may not have a degree and they are found in all walks of life, including, but certainly not only, academia.

Q: I have heard that there may be more than one kind of intelligence. Is this true?

A: In the 20th century, the research of Professor Howard Gardner, at the Harvard Graduate School of Education questioned the established idea that intelligence came in just one form that could be measured in an IQ test and that was that. Gardner's theory of *Multiple Intelligences* suggests that there may be at least seven different kinds of intelligences in humans, ranging from mathematical/logical to kinaesthetic (finely-tuned motor control and co-ordination). For example, a successful footballer might have kinaesthetic intelligence. A successful entrepreneur might have mathematical/logical intelligence. As you read this, you will be aware that it is perfectly possible for someone to be a successful entrepreneur *and* footballer all at the same time. In which case, they would have to have both kinaesthetic as well as mathematical/logical intelligence. Take a look at the sports news on any day and we see that there are examples of people who have combined business and sports careers successfully. Gardner's theory is continually developing. Notably, it has significantly opened up the debate about intelligence and taken research to another level in this field.

Q: Does having a high IQ guarantee that a person is going to achieve outstanding success in their chosen career?

A: No. Personality, health, individual creativity and environmental factors all have a role to play in what a person eventually achieves in life. Having a high IQ does not necessarily mean that a person will be outstanding in any given field. At the same time, however, having a high IQ does not preclude someone from being highly successful in any given area!

Q: What sorts of questions feature in IQ tests?

A: All IQ tests are united in trying to get a measure of intelligence, but *how* they achieve this can differ in the kinds of questions that are used in any given test. Initially, IQ tests derived from the work of European and North American psychologists. In lots of ways this is bad news. Whenever a test originates from a specific cultural context, unless steps are taken to ensure otherwise there is a danger that the questions are going to be culturally biased. In other words, the questions that feature in the test are no longer measuring intelligence, so much as what someone knows about a particular language and culture. Imagine, for example, having to take an intelligence test that required you to have a detailed knowledge of Yoruba language and culture in Nigeria. Unless you were familiar with these your score wouldn't be so hot! Obviously, any kind of test that is culturally biased produces a score that is unfair or inaccurate. In view of this, 'culture-fair' tests such as Raven's Progressive Matrices have become popular worldwide.

Raven's Standard Progressive Matrices Item A5

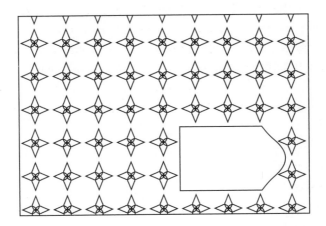

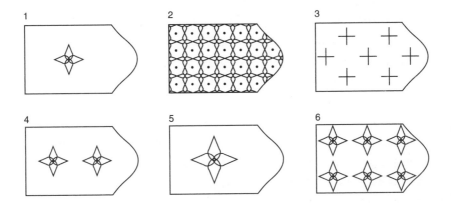

Item A5 courtesy of J. C. Raven Ltd

'Culture-fair' testing

The content of Raven's Standard Progressive Matrices, are image-based, as illustrated in the sample shown on page 23. How does the test work? Problem-solving questions are presented in a highly visual format, to enable your child to compare and contrast shapes and deduce patterns. I have found these tests to be particularly useful where a child's literacy may not be their strong point, but their independent thinking skills are!

CHECKPOINT

Q: Is literacy a test of ability?

A: No. Being able to read and write is one thing, individual intelligence and ability is another. Consider the following situation. Who would you rather have with you if were trapped at the top of Everest? A person who didn't know how to read and write but was an expert mountaineer, or a poet who liked mountains but knew nothing about climbing? I for one will take the former, please.

Literacy alone cannot determine a person's abilities. That is why culture-fair tests are so very important. The need for linguistic and specific cultural knowledge is kept to a minimum. By using abstract problems, presented by shapes and patterns, these tests guard against discrimination in cases where cultural background or linguistic ability may otherwise impair a person's score. So how do these tests compare with other intelligence tests that are used by education systems internationally? A look at the following tests provides the answer.

The Stanford Binet Intelligence Scale

This test takes part of its name from the French psychologist Alfred Binet, and part from Stanford University in the USA. It comprises a multiple IQ test, giving separate scores for:

◆ verbal (language ability);
◆ non-verbal (visual ability);
◆ mathematical;
◆ short-term memory ability.

Weschler Intelligence Scales

This test also provides separate scores for subtests which are each administered on their own. The topics that comprise the subtests are broad and include:

◆ a vocabulary test;
◆ an arithmetic test;
◆ problem-solving using pictures, words and wooden blocks.

Clearly, the Stanford Binet and Weschler Intelligence Scales are two very different tests, but they have some key features in common. Both tests:

◆ assume prior knowledge to answer verbal questions (for example, understanding certain random vocabulary may be needed for a child to be successful in a test);
◆ involve testing the memory in some way;
◆ don't particularly have a focus on testing thinking ability.

How much someone knows does not tell us anything about a child's individual ability other than that they have either a good memory, a good teacher or they are a good student – or all three! Put another way, both the Weschler and Standford Binet Scales do not really tell us a great deal about a child's independent thinking and creative ability. What are the implications for a child taking a test like this in real life? They could be full of energy, bright and raring to go but know very little about the topics that came up – for example, in the vocabulary section of the test. The result might be a low score which in no way reflects the true ability of the child. Hence, such tests can either be a hindrance or a help in discovering your child's full range of abilities.

In contrast, if it is independent thinking ability rather than knowledge you are interested in testing, then culture-fair tests discussed earlier, come out a clear winner. This is because the focus is not on trying to find out what your child does or doesn't happen to know. Rather, they are more geared to find out how they can use their independent thinking to find solutions to problems for themselves. And this makes a fairer ability test for every child.

Why does a thinking test make a fairer test?

Whichever school or city a child finds themselves in will determine what curriculum they are following and hence what they have learned at any given point. If a test is only going to take into account what a child is expected to know, based on only one kind of curriculum or place, then some children are going to come out better than others on the test simply because of where they live. By taking this risk out of the test, and focusing on testing individual thinking instead, it means that no matter which school or city they are in, or what curriculum they are following, a child is given a fair crack at it. Put another away, testing in such a way makes sure that the emphasis is not on trying to find out what your child doesn't know, but on *giving them the opportunity to let them show us what they can do.*

Sock it to me, Miss Smith!

However, as with any test forewarned is forearmed! The activities in sections III and IV not only take the lid off your child's thinking skills and creativity, they also provide practice in problem-solving and provide them with all the tricks they need to know to tackle these tests. So that if or when they *do* encounter a test, they will be confident in themselves and their abilities and be totally ready for it!

How to get the best out of test results

Love them or hate them, tests are firmly entrenched in education at present and when their results arrive home you need a game plan to make sure that your child gets as much as they can out of having done the test in the first place. How? Ask the school or person who administered the test a few hard and fast questions. The checklist below will ensure that you get all the answers that you want. And remember: don't be blinded by numbers and statistics, get to the bottom of how the test works and then you will know what it is actually measuring.

Checklist: Tests

✓ Which tests are your school using to determine your child's abilities?

✓ What is the content of the test?

✓ Is it mostly knowledge-based?

✓ Is the score given only an average?

✓ When the score is broken down, how did your child score on all the different parts of the test?

✓   Did they show a strength in any particular area (such as mathematics or vocabulary)?

✓   Has the school also used 'culture fair' tests based on more abstract problem-solving so that your child has had a chance to demonstrate their thinking ability?

These questions may seem to be nit-picking, but by getting the answers to them you are more likely to discover what your child has *actually* been tested for, what the scores really tell you and what children's individual strengths are. Average scores on a test are just that. They don't tell you how well your child scored on any specific part of a test. This goes not just for the tests discussed here but also university entrance tests, and annual or end of semester school diagnostic tests.

Depending on which country you are in when you are reading this book, schools will be using different ways of testing to measure your child's progress. It pays to know how they are doing this, and using the checklist above will ensure that you always get the best out of tests.

How much importance should we attach to test scores?

Tests have a role to play in helping us identify children's strengths, but they are just one way of trying to measure ability. That is all. There isn't a test in the world that can claim to be able to measure the full extent of your child's individual gifts and talents. All well-researched tests strive to be valid and reliable and are based on statistical averages. However, this can never change the fact that each child is unique, brilliant and beaming with their own individuality. You could say that if a child's potential knows no limits, tests are limited in their ability to capture that potential. Consider Einstein again for a moment. By all accounts of his genius in history it would have seemed that he should have sailed through his entrance test to higher education. But as we have learned, he didn't. Knowing what you do now from this chapter, this is perhaps no surprise at all, because the one thing Einstein had, that no test can claim to capture, was imagination.

How do you test imagination?

Einstein openly set more store in imagination than knowledge. His belief was that imagination above all else was the route of all progress. What might he have thought about a world where children are flooded with ability tests, none of which can claim to take imagination into account in their scores, and therefore do little to encourage a child's imagination to run free?

Brainbox

⚡   No test in the world can claim to be able to assess all your child's abilities – no matter how formal or official it may seem.

⚡   Intelligence tests can come in different formats.

⚡   Some intelligence tests are more 'culture fair' than others.

⚡   'Culture fair' means that they rely less upon a child having any particular knowledge to be able to do well on the test and more upon their independent thinking to solve abstract problems.

⚡   It's important to keep all tests in perspective in discovering a child's full range of gifts and talents. Remember, in da Vinci's day there weren't any!

Chapter 3

Your Child's Gifts

Rainbows of opportunity

The individual gifts of children are like the colours of a rainbow: no one can say where they begin or end, but they are there ready to be discovered and to shine. As every parent knows, every child's gifts are precious. Each child has their own personality and ways of telling you things. This means that some children's gifts can be elusive. The child may know they have a talent for something but are shy and secretive about it. Another child is happy to shout out what they are good at right away. Either way, this chapter is all about practical ways to help you discover your child's gifts.

Being a parent in the 21st century

You have already seen that parents were the foundation of Mozart, da Vinci and Einstein realizing their individual gifts and talents. But with no disrespect to our ancestors, I think it is fair to say that being a parent today has become considerably more wrought with new challenges specific to our era – the key one being time. I don't know about you, but I think all of us, our children included, are not far from being able to move at the speed of light

– we pack so much into each day! On the one hand the great thing about today is that we have a lot more knowledge available to us about our children and how they develop, think and learn. On the other hand, parents are bombarded with information, without the opportunity to decipher it and find out which bits might benefit their child. In an already busy life, we don't have the luxury of being able to sit down with someone, in the comfort of our own home, and just have them explain a few things, in a no-nonsense, down-to-earth way. Well relax, and grab a mug of your favourite tea. This chapter is about 'sitting down' with you, to provide you with the answers to some of the most frequently asked questions about a range of 'hot topics' for parents and their children today. Once you are armed with this knowledge you will be better placed, not only to help you discover more about your child's gifts, but more importantly how to help your child develop them in different ways.

FAQ

 Q: What do we mean by gifted and talented?

 A: During the latter half of the 20th century, schools worldwide developed an interest in gifts and talents. But depending on which country or education system you are talking about, the terms 'gifted' and 'talented' can mean the same or different things. In some countries, for example, gifted is used to mean those children who stand out in academic subjects, whereas talented is linked to ability in art, music or sport. Spot the problem? You might well ask, working within this definition, what happens to a *talented* football player, who is also *gifted* at heart surgery? Or Charlotte Church, world famous for her singing talent, but at the same gifted in academic subjects scoring brilliantly in her national examinations? Are these people gifted or talented? In reality they are, of course, both!

Labels and definitions are neat and tidy – children's abilities are not

Since time immemorial children have always defied theories and any attempt to pigeon-hole their abilities. Imagine trying to separate out Leonardo da Vinci's mixture of scientific, musical and artistic abilities into either being gifted or talented and quickly you find yourself in a bit of a muddle.

My advice? Stay clear of labels. Remain focused on the one fact that you know to be true. Every child is an original, as unique as their thumb print. They are not a national average computed by some whiz bang pop statistical calculation. 'Catch all' definitions that put a ring around children's abilities are wonderful for filing systems. But in practice, the terms 'gifted', 'talented', 'gifts', 'talents', 'abilities' and 'genius' only become truly meaningful in the precise context of individual children themselves. So, here is to helping your child develop their individual gifts – one and all of them!

FAQs

  Q: What is creativity?

  A: You have probably noticed that creativity is *the* 'buzz' word of the 21st century. So what is all the fuss about? The term 'creativity' can be used in two different ways. On the one hand we can talk about creativity as being the mental ability to think creatively. On the other hand we can see creativity as a kind of energy at work inside us. When someone develops a new business idea, or writes a piece of music, paints a picture, or designs something new and innovative we see that energy at work. Creativity lies somewhere in between a person's imagination and their own individual abilities. Anyone who tries to tell you they know any more about creativity than that either doesn't understand what they are talking about or is trying to blind you with science. All indications are that we are probably not even scratching the surface of the creativity we each have inside us. The following research is a case in point.

Finding hidden creativity

In 2002, at the Centre for the Mind in Sydney, Australia, Professors Elaine Mulcahy and Allan Snyder conducted an experiment to see what would happen to people's creativity when their brains were stimulated with magnetism. The adults selected for the experiment all had good physical and mental health, but displayed no particular creative ability. The results were amazing. After their brains had been magnetized, for a short time – no more than 15 minutes – they displayed extraordinary artistic ability, creating drawings of tremendous talent. The findings suggested that somehow magnetizing the brain had set free hidden creativity. It is not yet fully understood how or why this happened, but the experiment demonstrated that whereas the people involved had not thought themselves to be particularly creative, somewhere in their mind lay the potential to be *extremely* creative.

Needless to say, sticking a fridge magnet to your head is not recommended! There are plenty of ways to unlock your child's creativity and none of them described in this book includes the use of fridge magnets. So do not share this bit of research with your child unless you want to suffer the consequences. You have been warned!

☼ **Q:** Are children naturally creative?

☼ **A:** Yes. Children are bubbling with creative energy!

☼ **Q:** Creative 'types' are those people you find in arts, music and drama, aren't they?

A: No! Those are people who demonstrate creativity in these fields, but it is a popular misconception that they are the *only* creative 'types' around. It does not matter what field a person is in, from being a dancer, gardener, lawyer, to entrepreneur. Creativity is found in every field. In a sense it is the individual creativity of people in all walks of life that drives everything forward.

Q: What can we do to help children develop their creativity?

A: Give them plenty of opportunities to use it, and explore it, starting with the activities in this book.

Q: Can creativity be measured?

A: There are tests for creativity but none of them are foolproof. This is because the point at which individual creativity begins or ends in a person cannot be measured. One of the most established creativity tests challenges a person to come up with as many different ideas as they can about something. For example, '*How many uses can you find for a brick*'? is a classic creativity test question. The tester then marks the person's creativity by counting how many different ideas they came up with. What sometimes stops both children and adults from scoring as highly as they might do on such a test is that they don't really let their thinking go wild enough. What do I mean? If we are not used to regularly letting all our ideas out and openly expressing them, when presented with a question such as this, we can put a block on our thinking. We may stick to the conventional ways we have seen bricks used, keeping us in our comfort zone so we feel safe. Anywhere beyond that point, we feel our ideas are a bit 'wacky'. The trick is to have confidence in our ideas, and let them roll.

Creativity and genius

Creativity, like imagination and individual ability, is therefore another of those things that defies measurement but which we know features greatly in the works of Mozart, da Vinci and Einstein. None of their achievements were the same, and they each explored different areas of interest. But what united them is that they each found their own way to unlock their individual creativity and make it work for them. An integral part of Thumb Print Learning® is to give children the opportunity to do this for themselves. As they complete the activities in the following chapters, they will discover their own creativity and develop confidence in their ideas. No 'brick' question will ever stump *them*! But before that, what about your child's gifts and how can you discover them?

Gifts come in all kinds of packages

Our children are each such a heady mixture of individual personalities, emotions, talents, ideas and creativity that their gifts aren't always obvious. Add into the equation hormones, if your child is reaching puberty, and their gifts can become buried under a sea of trips to doctors to sort out their acne, dealing with hairs that sprouted overnight, or the embarrassment of their voice dropping two octaves whilst they were answering a question in class. So, here are a few signs and symptoms to help you identify your child's individual gifts.

- **The Leader**: Outgoing personality, takes the lead naturally, from school projects to class discussions. Always has done, ever since they were in kindergarten and took it upon themselves to reorganize the other children in the Wendy house – when they were three.

- **The Thinker**: Great ideas, but shy personality, so doesn't take the lead in projects, and then quietly smoulders inside when they see their idea was 'tons' better than everyone else's, and they should have spoken up.

- **The Tycoon**: Isn't too hot on homework unless it involves something that excites them, captures their imagination and gives them a chance to be innovative and share ideas. Has already figured out a way that the school could be run better and actually make a profit. Turned their pocket money into a bank when they were six.

- **The Enigma**: Finds attractive and enjoyable what might seem to others complex, such as doing puzzles, fixing the dishwasher when it is broken and everyone else has given up (!), or finding the answer to *that* really tough question at school.

- **The Pop Star**: Openly displays their creative energy in any given area. This could be expressed in any way they feel free and able to do so. From the way they dance, do their hair, decorate their bedroom, present their work at school, to how they make their first million, aged 12, with a new hit song.

- **The Mature Conversationalist (Natterbox)**: Reads widely and can tell you something about almost anything. Never seems to take a breath when they are talking. Outstripping the knowledge of their peers, they can prefer conversations with older children and/or adults. Never get into a debate or argument with them – as you know – they *always* win.

- **The Sophisticate**: Likes learning and a challenge. With the quiet poise of a Siamese cat, chews up (supposedly) challenging homework, in just under six seconds. Then looks at their nails, yawns, and complains of boredom. Can be four going on 14.

- **The Fidget**: Likes learning and a challenge. With the tail-wagging enthusiasm of a Labrador puppy gobbles up (supposedly) challenging homework, in just under six seconds. Then shouts, grinning: '*Next!*' If nothing arrives, starts teasing the cat and fidgets with boredom. Can be 14 going on four.

- **The Entertainer**: Sometimes, (well, quite often actually), gets into mischief in lessons at school because they can read the teacher's mind, pre-empt their every word, and thus run rings round them every day (pity the teacher). Likes strategy games, such as chess, and competitive sports. Loves to win. Rarely loses.

- **The Visionary**: Can just 'switch off' and tune out. Creates doodles that end up looking like a painting by Michelangelo or designs for everything and anything, from a new laptop to a revolutionary car. Does all this in the gaps they have left in lessons when they finished their work ages ago and the teacher hasn't yet noticed.

- **The Dazzler**: This year, won both the mathematics *and* poetry writing contest at school. Won the science competition last year too. Captains a sports team for the school and the violin lessons are going very well. Landed the lead part in the school play (again). They are rarely invited to other kid's birthday parties. Their parents are puzzled by this.

These signs and symptoms of individual ability could never be exhaustive. They are not intended to be, nor are they meant to be used prescriptively. More likely is that each child will have a mixture of gifts, some of which are, and some of which are not to be found in these profiles.

The purpose of this exercise was to let you see this wide range of signs and symptoms of individual gifts *before* I let you in on a secret. All or any combination of them indicates not only that your child has individual gifts, but that they may be *exceptionally* brilliant, or have the potential to be out-standing, in one or more subject areas. We smile with pleasure and marvel at our children's gifts often without realizing what they *really* mean. So, for example, the *Sophisticate* is not so much 'good at homework' as completely under-challenged at school, the *Entertainer* is not so much mischievous, as they are such a quick thinker that they find it more of a challenge to outwit the teacher than actually do the work that is set in class. As I said earlier, gifts come in all kinds of packaging, and depending on the wrapping, they are not always so obvious.

Mistaken identities

It may have already dawned on you that if the symptoms and signs given here are not seen for what they *really* are: natural gifts to be developed, they could easily be misconstrued as anything from hyperactivity, hormonal problems (for older children), inability to concentrate, laziness, to 'problems with authority'. Depending on the strategies different children use to cope with their school day, their gifts can be buried or highlighted. For example, I have found extremely bright children in both 'bottom sets' and 'top sets' in schools. The only difference between them was how they handled boredom in lessons. One child would keep quiet about the fact that they were bored, whereas another was more verbal, and let everyone know about how they felt, including the teacher. No prizes for guessing which one ended up in 'bottom set' – regardless how bright they were. This doesn't mean that the quieter one was any better off, though. Sure, they were in top set, but they were still bored. Nor does it mean that it is OK for a child to take out their frustration on a teacher. The message here is that, if a child's gifts slip through the net, everyone loses out, and no one more than the child them-self. Before going on to discuss how you can work with schools to make sure that none of *your* child's gifts slip through the net, it is important to consid-er other instances where individual ability can easily go unnoticed.

Special educational needs and genius

Dyslexia

Research into possible links between dyslexia and genius is ongoing, but it is clear that no child with dyslexia is precluded from being a genius. Leonardo da Vinci is a case in point. We cannot know for sure whether or not he was dyslexic, but from the material he left us, it is certain that the letters in his notes emulate what can be a sign of dyslexia: all his letters are reversed. As we all know, this certainly didn't stop him from having brilliant ideas. Indeed, some research argues that it may have been his dyslexic ability that was a major factor that contributed to his gift for visualizing his ideas in such detail, and recreating them in his drawings so vividly.

Autism

Unless you have encountered autism yourself, you may only have a vague idea about what it is. It is a spectrum of conditions, in which a child can also have what are known as *islets of ability*. These islets are very special indeed and make the rest of our efforts pall into insignificance in the kinds of creativity they often display. If you are unfamiliar with the kind of thing I am talking about here, you may recall the film *Rainman* starring Dustin Hoffman, whose character had a fantastic ability in mathematics and arithmetic that enabled him to work out in his head the odds of winning in casino games. This kind of thing is not impossible for children or adults with autism. From a very young age, the world-famous artist Steven Wiltshire was not only able to draw, but also produced sketches which commanded a complete understanding of perspective, architecture and dimension – a maturity in ability that otherwise can take years to develop to the degree of accuracy exhibited in his work. Tending to mix these high levels of creative ability with a difficulty in being able to form empathy with others, the condition remains a perplexing one. However, research to date suggests that genius and autism are not mutually exclusive. Indeed, where I have run summer enrichment programmes (which are discussed again later in this chapter, *see* page 46), children with autism have attended and taken part in full. While not all children with autism are comfortable around lots of people they are unfamiliar with, as is the scenario with a summer school programme, the children with autism I have known have handled it very well, and attended programmes voluntarily. It all depends on the individual child. So, if your child does have autism, depending upon how comfortable they feel around other people, enrichment programmes are definitely worth exploring.

Obviously the guidance given here on children with special educational needs can only be general – it is not intended to be otherwise – and cannot replace a specific diagnosis of your child's abilities. However, the main point to be taken is that while there is much research still to be done, there are clearly some huge areas of potential overlap between what might be construed as genius and children with special educational needs.

Working with schools

All schools are there to help your child, and in my experience most schools spend a great deal of time and effort toward this end. Communicating with schools can be hampered by the fact that we live in such a time-starved world. However, if your child has any or all of the 'symptoms' discussed above, and you want to be certain that your school is aware of them, you need to be able to make the most of any meetings that you have with your child's school. The following checklist is there to help you do this.

Checklist: your child's gifts at school

✓   Find out if the school is aware of the full range of your child's gifts that you have discovered either from this chapter or otherwise. Parent's evenings are the best time to do this as you, your child and teachers are all present, creating the opportunity for open and positive discussion.

✓   Using what you learned about tests in chapter 2, ask them to show you the kind of tests the school has used to determine your child's abilities. (Remember that averages are less useful than breaking down the test scores to find your child's strengths.)

✓   Are there any other factors that you need to take into consideration that may be helping or hindering your child's performance at school – for example, relationships with peers and teachers.

✓   If children are in their teens, remind teachers (as well as yourself!) that those wonderful things called hormones need to be taken into account, especially when looking at current behaviour and attitude patterns.

✓   Remember that teachers are there to help and advise, and are with your child five days a week. Working together you have a better chance of coming up with a winning plan for your child's success.

✓   Once you and your child are happy that no stone has been left unturned, and that you have worked out a good plan of action with your school, set a date to review how the plan is going and/or make any adjustments at that time.

Involving your child

Involving your child, whether in junior or high school, in the above process to build a plan of action for their success is vital. It empowers your child with a sense that they are not only the subject of the plan, they are a joint creator of it. In other words, no one is telling them what to do for the best. Right from the start, they have been consulted, put their ideas forward and have agreed a plan that *they* are happy with. Imposing a regime on anyone, children included, never did anyone any good. All that happens is that they revolt, throw tantrums and you end up in conflict (as you know that goes for adults too!). Involve your child in building their *own* plan and they are beginning to take responsibility for their own progress. Plus, when and if they have a bad day, they cannot turn around and blame it all on you. After all they helped hammer out the plan and agreed to it, right? Right.

CHECKPOINT

Q: But what do you do if, even after working out a super plan with the school, your child comes home regularly complaining that they are feeling under-challenged – alright, bored!

A: In some cases a child may benefit from acceleration and/or enrichment programmes. Although practiced throughout the world acceleration remains a controversial topic and requires careful thinking. So what are acceleration and enrichment programmes? How do they work? And what are the advantages and disadvantages of these programmes for children? All of these questions are answered for you next.

Acceleration and enrichment programmes

Acceleration programmes

Acceleration as the name suggests means allowing children the opportunity to move on at their own speed, and leapfrog conventional stages in their education. What happens when they do? The story of Ruth Lawrence provides some insight into what can be gained by children taking the acceleration route.

Ruth Lawrence

As other children her age were still in school, Ruth began a mathematics degree at Oxford University. Since she had been a baby, Ruth had been taught mathematics by her father at home. While still a child, Ruth's father prepared and entered her for public mathematics examinations ordinarily geared for teenagers. Ruth excelled in all of them to win her place at Oxford.

Ruth Lawrence's academic achievements are without doubt brilliant. However, had Ruth gone through the more conventional school route, would she have been able to achieve what she did when she did? In other words, whatever her own individual mathematical ability may have been from the start, Ruth's success in gaining a place at Oxford before her teens was gained openly via the support and encouragement of her family, and by following a period of one-to-one study with her father in which the primary focus was mathematics.

Today, there are more established and formal ways of doing what Ruth did over 20 years ago. A list of universities that offer acceleration programmes for parents, schools and children around the world is given at the end of this book. However, before you decide this could be something you would like to consider for your child, here are some 'pros and cons' that I recommend you think about first.

PROS

★   If a child is so far ahead of the others in their class in any subject, then it makes sense for everyone for acceleration to be considered. Think of the child Mozart working through conventional music lessons in your local school and you can see where acceleration may be something that could make practical sense – for everyone.

★   The child can move at their own natural pace and so boredom is less likely to set in.

★   They will be able to mix with people of a very different age to them – at university, for example.

★   Where a child would enjoy this experience, is comfortable with this outcome and wants to do it, they can be very happy.

CONS

✦   A child may not want to be accelerated because they like things the way they are!

✦   They feel confident that they will still be able to achieve their goals without moving quicker than they are currently through school.

✦   They don't particularly like the idea of being surrounded by people who are all older than them; they would like to go to university later.

For a child reaching for the moon and stars, there are always at least two routes to their dreams. Whether your child is accelerated or not, it doesn't change the fact that they are brilliant, and can achieve what they want whichever route they choose. If they do want to consider acceleration then you need to explore all the options carefully.

Checklist: acceleration

✓   Discuss acceleration with your child's school.

✓   Work out a plan whereby your child can try out a programme of acceleration, and then either continue or discontinue it depending on how they feel.

✓   Make sure you have a flexible enough system in place that has an 'out clause', and keeps all options open.

✓   Acceleration can work, but only where the child is totally aware of all of the factors involved, and is happy with what it will entail. The best advice I can give is this: ask your child what they want to do, and work forward from there.

Enrichment programmes

Enrichment overlaps with acceleration in that it is another opportunity for children to develop their gifts outside the normal school timetable. But enrichment programmes are not so much about accelerating learning. More precisely, enrichment programmes are about enabling your child to explore a topic in more depth and breadth than normally might be achievable within normal school hours.

Schools often build enrichment into their school year, but you might not know it as 'enrichment'. However, you have probably heard of school trips to the theatre, geography field trips or language exchange programmes. These are all forms of enrichment.

Summer schools are another long-established form of enrichment. These are sometimes offered by universities in conjunction with schools to provide children with further learning opportunities in a range of subject areas. Further information on international programmes for both acceleration and enrichment can be found in the end section of this book.

Hoisting the flag as we arrive at base camp

We have come a long way since chapter 1. We have exploded myths about genius, got inside tests and their scores, found out about your child's gifts and discovered that your child shares in common with da Vinci, Mozart, and Einstein three *natural* abilities, none of which can be measured or captured by a test, and all of which we can develop ourselves. I like to call them the Three 'A's of Genius.

★   Ability to think creatively, and independently;
★   Ability to learn – which, thanks to each of our fantastic brains, is limitless;
★   Ability to develop our own individual way of thinking and learning.

Our journey to this point has been a fast and furious one, but as you arrive at the end of this chapter and section you now see genius unravelled, tests brought down to size, and the brilliance of your child's natural abilities. The parents of da Vinci, Mozart and Einstein started off pretty much where you are at now, only minus the knowledge you have at your disposal in this and the following two sections. Their children began as your child begins now: as a young person with their own unique gifts and unlimited potential – an apprentice in their own development. Helping your child to unleash their own natural gifts and creativity, and showing them how to think and learn like a genius starts here!

Brainbox

- ① Think about your child's gifts like the merging colours of a rainbow and the possibilities are endless.
- ① There are a whole range of 'symptoms' that can demonstrate that your child's creativity and thinking is not being appropriately challenged; boredom is often a key indicator of this – so it is worth taking seriously any comments your child might make about being bored!
- ① Special educational needs and genius are not mutually exclusive.
- ① 'Gifted' and 'talented' are words we hear used in the media often. Depending on which country they are used in, these can be used interchangeably or to refer to different kinds of abilities. 'Gifted' can be used to refer to academic ability, and 'talented' to creative arts and sports. But given that these kinds of abilities can often overlap, it doesn't pay to get too hung up on terms!
- ① Labels are neat and tidy, children's abilities are not.
- ① All children are born with three natural abilities that provide them with the potential to think like a genius – the abilities to think, to learn and to develop their own individual way of thinking and learning.

section three

How to Think Like a Genius

Chapter 4

What Makes Great Thinkers,

Great Thinkers?

Thinking is a fabulous thing; we do it all the time without thinking about it! But 'thinking about thinking' is one of those tricks of genius that makes some people not just good, but *great* thinkers. So how do they do it? By the end of this chapter you will have learned how to do this. They will be able to tap consciously into this ability any time they want or need to. So what is 'thinking about thinking'? How does it work?

Metacognition – big word simple meaning

The term used for this mental process of 'thinking about thinking' is 'metacognition'. It derives from Greek and Latin words meaning:

meta: change + *cognition*: knowing

When I am introducing metacognition in seminars, I usually take a small pause at this point. This is because both the term and what it means are not concepts that we often use in our everyday conversations. We do not exactly spring out of bed in the morning and think: '*I wonder how my metacognition is doing today!*' So we need some quick 'jargon busting' here to get to the crunch of why 'thinking about thinking' makes great thinkers, great thinkers. And why being aware of, and consciously using this thinking ability, can help your child to 'think like a genius'. The pause in the seminars creates some time to do this, and in the process gives participants a chance to ask some questions. So let's take a pause and jump straight in.

FAQs

☀ **Q:** Is thinking about thinking a *natural* mental capacity?

☀ **A:** Yes! It's a natural part of how our brains work. But most of the time we don't consciously call upon this natural ability because we aren't aware that it exists. Knowing how to tap into this ability consciously is what can make the difference between accidentally having great thoughts and ideas, and being able to use this mental power on demand.

☀ **Q:** Are there some individuals who are particularly good at it?

☀ **A:** Yes. People who achieve outstanding things in their given field often demonstrate good metacognitive ability. So great minds really do think alike!

☀ **Q:** Can we learn how to get better at doing this for ourselves?

☀ **A:** Yes. We can all develop our thinking strategies by learning and being aware of different patterns of thinking. By keeping our minds open to new ways of seeing, thinking and learning, we enable ourselves to maximize our thinking ability.

Q: Is it hard to learn how to 'think about thinking'?

A: No. Like most things in life, it's easy when you know how. And that is what this chapter is all about: showing your child how to tap into this natural ability and discover and develop it for themselves.

Q: How does the development of metacognition make people great thinkers?

A: Great thinkers capitalize upon this mental power in any situation they are presented with. They are therefore very effective thinkers. Imagine someone had just handed you a puzzle and you had never seen anything like it before in your life. In order to solve the puzzle you would first have to understand it. To do that, you would have to keep exploring parts of the puzzle, switching thinking strategies in response to what you discovered, and rotating your thoughts until you understood it better. Then you could solve the puzzle. The ability to do all of this, at great speed, is what great thinkers do. This is finely tuned metacognition working in practice.

Q: Is teaching children how to develop their thinking new to the 21st century?

A: No! As far back as ancient Greece, thinking was considered an important part of the learning process. In the Middle Ages children who were fortunate enough to have tutors, such as the princes and princesses of Europe, were taught how to think via philosophy and to question what they learned critically. After years of focusing upon knowledge gathering, and testing, learning how to think has gradually fallen by the wayside with the advent of mass education systems. Gradually governments are addressing this – they have no choice. The importance of not only being able to learn knowledge, but think independently has been highlighted by the global knowledge economy. Developing thinking skills in our children today should be as natural to them as being taught how to brush their teeth. By the end of this chapter for your child, it will be!

So, how does 'thinking about thinking' work to benefit us in practice? The story of the Apollo 13 mission provides an excellent example of how being able to consciously tap into this natural mental energy can produce extraordinary thinking.

When thinking about thinking counts – 'OK Houston, we have a problem'

In 1970 the Apollo 13 rocket shot into space to fly to the moon. As history and the Hollywood film of the same name dramatically illustrated, reaching the Moon on the Apollo 13 space mission was not meant to be. But out of this adversity came some spectacular and successful thinking.

Jim Lovell was the astronaut and captain of the mission. At first all seemed to go well. Apollo 13 managed its ascent into space and the crew of astronauts could see the Moon clearly. But then they ran into trouble. Problems had developed. Substantial power had been lost in the space capsule, at the same time causing the oxygen supply for the crew to become depleted. Combined, these problems meant that not only would Apollo 13 and its crew not reach the moon on this mission, the possibility that they may not get back to Earth in one piece became a real and frightening one. Jim Lovell contacted Houston with the words now immortalized in history, and possibly the biggest understatement of the 20th century: 'OK Houston, we have a problem.'

Gene Kranz was the 'man on the ground' at NASA, whose job it was to bring back Apollo 13 and its crew safely. He acted quickly and calmly. He knew there was a problem but the question was how to solve it.

A huge amount of the NASA team's time prior to the event had been dedicated to thinking and working to one precise objective. Their job had been to design a specific type of rocket with a specific set of components for a specific job: landing a crew of astronauts on the Moon. The focus had now switched to a different objective, saving a crew in a damaged craft and bringing them home. The NASA team had to change their thinking – and quick.

Gene Kranz began to attack the problem by getting his team to brainstorm rapidly. Breaking the problem down into its components, they began working on how to find a solution. The word solution is important here. Gene Kranz set his team up to believe in their mental ability to crack the problem and find a solution right from the start. Minutes before his team set off to find solutions, as he recalls in his book *Failure is not an option*, he set his team up to find a successful solution for Apollo 13. He began by clearly communicating to his team, the positive mindset he wanted them to attack the problem in: *'I don't give a damn about the odds and I don't give a damn that we've never done anything like this before … this crew is coming home. Now let's get going!'* As we all know it worked. Gene Kranz and his team cracked an extraordinarily difficult problem with great success, and brought the crew home safely.

What enabled the NASA team to think like this? What brilliant mental activity were they tapping into during the whole event? They were using their metacognitive ability to problem-solve a critical situation. The Apollo 13 team at NASA were involved in changing, rotating and adjusting their thinking strategies (meta activity), in order to figure out (cognitive activity) how to return the Apollo 13 craft and team (problem-solving activity) safely back to Earth. Working our metacognition – works!

CHECKPOINT

Q: **So what is the difference between metacognition and problem-solving?**

A: **In a nutshell, if metacognition is our inbuilt ability to adapt and rotate our thinking, problem-solving is about learning how to *apply* this mental activity consciously to *specific* situations.**

Importantly, if children are made aware that they have this natural mental power, and they know how best to apply it in problem-solving situations, they stand a better chance of being successful in finding solutions.

Rocket scientists need not apply

The Apollo 13 team at NASA had to rethink their strategies on how to save a spacecraft and people's lives, under the watchful eyes of the world and under tremendous time pressures. Thankfully, most of us do not have to do this kind of thinking under that kind of pressure. But it is both being aware of this natural ability *and* being able to consciously tap into it, as and when we want to, that creates a foundation for developing great thinking habits. And we don't need to be rocket scientists to be able to use this fabulous mental power.

Although mostly we use this natural thinking power subconsciously, one of the situations that can make us tap into it more effectively – but usually without realizing it – is an emergency. Every year, anywhere in the world, we hear amazing stories of people who became trapped by the forces of nature and yet managed to survive against all the odds. What makes these stories so fascinating to the media and to all of us is that they are not about rocket scientists, film stars or celebrities, they are about *ordinary people* who had planned to do an *ordinary* activity, such as a family holiday or a day out in the countryside. A sudden change in weather, an injury – or both – forced them into a situation where their natural mental abilities were pushed to the fore. The consequence? They achieved brilliant results. In short, the emergency acted as a release button in their thinking, causing them to focus, concentrate, block out everything else, and keep rotating and adjusting their thinking until they came up with a genius strategy to save their lives.

So how can we make our children more aware of this natural gift of thinking so that they can consciously tap into it – *without* having to go through such an emergency! We can start by celebrating that most natural ability they possess: Curiosity!

Why 'why questions' are good!

Asking questions is one of the things that makes children so brilliant. And they do it to us when and where we least expect it:

♦   'Why is my brother in your belly, Mum?'
♦   'Why do dogs have tails?'
♦   'Where does the sun hide at night?'
♦   'Where did I come from?'
♦   'Where does the Earth come from? Oh, right, the universe ... so where does that come from, Daddy?'

These are the sorts of questions young children are always asking. I say young children, because as we move up into our adolescence 'why questions' have a tendency to become more associated with requests like: 'Why can't I have that new pair of designer trainers, Mum?' 'Why can't I stay out all night at the rock concert?' Our children's lifestyle demands aside (!), 'why questions' are good. They involve our children in an upward spiral of thinking activity which:

★   Harnesses natural curiosity to explore new topics
★   Develops natural metacognitive ability

★   Improves logic and reasoning
★   Enables children to learn to articulate their own individual thoughts
     and ideas.

Don't give them the answer!

Our instincts are to help our children. Like busy birds in spring we fly to and from our houses providing for them. So when they ask a 'why question' the automatic response is to try to give them the answer. Giving them the answer is fine, it develops one kind of mental activity very well – knowledge gathering. But what is the use of gathering lots of knowledge about unconnected things if we don't then know how to apply it? In other words, what about developing their *thinking* through this natural 'why questioning' process also? What if every once in a while we say to them: '*What do you think the answer is*?' '*Why do you think that*?' '*How is that then*?' Intersperse this with some 'knowledge sharing' between you and them, to help them learn more, and some reasoning time to allow them to develop their logic. By engaging in this kind of 'thinking conversation' they would be able to develop their independent thinking and learning ability into the bargain. Wouldn't that be a stroke of genius? That is exactly what the Greek philosopher Socrates thought when he came up with the idea somewhere between the 5th and 4th centuries CE.

Socrates decided that 'downloading' information to his pupils, and treating them as passive receivers of knowledge, was not a very effective method of learning. It did not engage the mind of the students and so they became bored and lost interest. But if they were engaged in a free-flowing conversation with their teacher, they were involved in a far more fruitful and exciting activity. By being active participants in a 'thinking conversation' they were encouraged to tap into their own thoughts about a topic, questioning and learning as they went along. *Through this mix of thinking and learning they came to know facts for themselves*. In the process, they also learned to reason, articulate their reasoning and to think the logic of ideas through for themselves. Brilliant! So how can children get started on learning about this for themselves?

Activity 1: The Why Tree

The Why Tree is a fun, effective, ready-to-use activity, grounded in the Socratic method. It has purposely been designed to be 'child friendly' to enable children, whatever their age, to become accustomed to harnessing their natural curiosity to develop their thinking and metacognitive ability. By teaching your child how to take charge of their own thinking when they discover a new topic, you empower them to understand concepts and ideas from 'the inside out'. This helps them:

★   Think through topics for themselves;
★   Make links between what they already know and new topics;
★   Have the confidence to explore topics in their own way, using their own ideas.

Taken together, developing these skills help our children to finely tune their metacognitive ability, and at the same time keep their natural curiosity alive.

How to help children get the best out of this activity

Choose absolutely any topic, grab a 'thought branch', decide who is going to ask the first question (you or your child) and then follow where the thought branch takes you! The thought branches can go on for as far you want them to. It doesn't matter whether you are thinking about a star fish, DNA or an orange – and it can be done absolutely anywhere, anytime. You

The Why Tree

will be amazed where Why Tree conversations can take you! You may find that your child takes hold of a topic and wants to learn more after you finish the activity. A major spin off here is that children learn the power of being independent thinkers and learners. They see that there are no limits to where their thinking can take them. Enjoy!

Here's an example, using the 'thought branch' topic of Rainbows.

Child: What makes a rainbow like it is?

Adult: It's made from water and sunlight.

C: How can that be?

A: You can get colours from water.

C: When? I have never seen those colours in water.

A: What colour would you say water is then?

C: I don't know, grey?

A: Why do you think it is grey?

C: Well, because it doesn't have much of a colour …

A: Why do you think we can see things through water?

C: Because water is clear more than grey, it doesn't have much of a colour; yes, I'd say it's because it is 'see through', it isn't really grey, it just doesn't have a colour.

A: What if I told you that when light is split up it turns into different colours?

C: When could that happen!?

A: When light passes through things that are clear it can get split up!

C: How?

A: When light passes through things, it can bounce off different surfaces, and when it does, it makes different colours. That's what makes a diamond shine so beautifully, all the light is bouncing around inside it and making different colours!

C: Why is that happening in the sky though?

A: Rainbows happen when there is water in the air. After a big storm for example, just as the clouds clear, and the sun comes out, there

	is still a lot of water in the air in small droplets.
C:	Where does the rainbow come from then – the storm?
A:	Well, sort of. Remember the light bouncing through the diamond? The light from the sun shines through the small droplets of water left after the storm. Imagine that each of the small droplets of water is like a tiny diamond. What do you think happens when the sunlight passes through the tiny droplets of water?
C:	The light bounces around making different colours!
A:	Yes, that's right, that's how a rainbow happens …

Depending not on their age, but the level of understanding a child wants to explore with this topic, you can adjust the depth of questioning to take them as far along the thought branch as *they* feel happy with. For example, the child may be happy to stop at the idea that rainbows are caused by light passing through droplets of water, and pick the topic up another time. On the other hand, they might want to explore further how the rays of light from the sun are refracted through the droplets of water to make the rainbow. They may go on to find out about refraction for themselves. Remember, the 'Why Tree' can take them wherever they want to go. And that is the point. The floodgates are wide open for your child to pursue their own thoughts, ideas, questions, logic and reasoning. Being more aware of their own brain power in this way, they become masters of their own learning.

With time and practice the Why Tree helps children build confidence in their own thinking ability, and shows them that they don't have to wait to be told about anything; no matter what it is they can find it out for themselves by exercising their own mental power. The Why Tree has an insatiable appetite for new knowledge, so don't be surprised if your child finds out about new topics that interest them and uses the technique to teach *you* about them.

CHECKPOINT

Notice that throughout the rainbows example above, the emphasis is not so much on the answer, but *how* we get there: engaging the child's curiosity, reasoning and questioning to arrive at their new bit of knowledge – *together!*

What would happen if we had started this activity by giving them the definition of a rainbow: 'rainbows are rays of sunlight being refracted through droplets of moisture'? If you started with that, depending upon the child's previous knowledge, you might then have to unpack the meanings of everything you had just said. And this would work very well. As long as you remember to:

★   Let *them* do the unpacking with you;
★   Provide your child with the opportunity to use their logic, questions and reasoning to guide the process forward;
★   Resist the temptation just to give them 'the answer'.

FAQ

 Q: What's the difference between this kind of activity and brainstorming?

 A: Brainstorming can be an individual activity, but typically it is a group problem-solving activity with the objective of generating ideas in order to reach a specified end point. (For example, the Apollo 13 NASA team trying to bring a damaged space capsule back to earth safely, as demonstrated earlier). Here both the activity and the objective are different. This activity is not about putting a limit on your child's thinking by pre-setting a specific end point, or about them generating ideas to reach that specific end point.

What *is* emphasized is your child feeling free to keep pursuing a thought branch as far as *they* want to. In this sense the end point is infinity. The important point is not where your child gets to, but *how* they get there – *via the process of thinking for themselves.*

Seeing different things in different ways

The Why Tree, used regularly, teaches children how to use their curiosity, develop their thinking and use their ability to question and reason when they learn. All of this helps to develop that all important feature of great thinkers: metacognitive ability.

But to make our metacognitive ability work hard for us, we need to tap into another gift we all have – the ability to step back from something so that we can see it in different ways. When we do this it helps the metacognitive process by helping us to rotate our thoughts in order to work out solutions to new challenges, situations or problems.

Artists have played on this natural mental ability to see things in different ways since ancient times. For example, look at the pictures on page 64, and see the images 'pop in and out' depending on where you position yourself to view them. But we don't have to look at these carefully crafted images to realize that there are at least two ways of seeing anything. And that not everyone will see everything in the same way, all of the time.

Remember looking at a fluffy cloud against a clear blue sky on a bright summer day, or a smoky shadow on a wall at night in a dimly lit room, and pronouncing it was a rabbit, only for someone else to argue it was a bird? At first you may not have seen that it could also be 'their' bird as well as 'your' rabbit, but then when they explain *how* they got their idea you see it too. Remember too coming home from school, finding the house quiet, and grabbing that hairbrush, spoon or mum's favourite piece of porcelain, holding the item in front of your lips, and singing passionately into your new 'microphone' in front of the mirror?

Seeing Different Things in Different Ways

Are the horizontal lines parallel or do they slope?

Can you see the three faces?

Keeping this ability fresh and alive in children to see in different ways is a foundation of great thinking. Below is an activity to help them to be more aware of and maximize on this natural ability to solve unfamiliar problems or answer unfamiliar questions. This combined with the activities in the next chapter, is good preparation for children before doing ability tests. (To revise or see ability tests for the first time, *see* chapter 2.) Sometimes, because situations presented in tests look unfamiliar, a child can see no way around them. And yet, using a simple strategy such as this, they would be able to see the problem in a different way. Seeing the problem in a different way teaches them that they are able to *think* about the problem in a different way. This provides them with a technique to find their own way 'into' the problem. Then they can start to figure it out. Finely tuned metacognition in action!

Only Two Square Windows?

How many square windows can you see in this house?

Activity 2: Only Two Square Windows

This activity enables your child to see the benefits of thinking about what they see before them in different ways. It asks your child: 'How many square windows can you see in the house?' The answer is 60 altogether. How? Each of the two large square windows are divided up into smaller squares. Different patterns of squares emerge depending on how we think about and group the individual squares in the windows. Each of the windows has 30 'squares' when we look at the windows in the following ways:

◆   A window made up of 1 large square (×1).
◆   A window made up of 16 individual squares (×16).
◆   A window with 4 squares, each containing 9 squares (×4). To see this you have to let yourself see each 'window' not as a set of compartmentalized squares, but overlapping areas of squares.
◆   A window with 9 squares, of four squares each (×9). To see this we can start a number of different ways. Here is one way. We can bisect the window vertically and horizontally making four quarters. Each of these squares comprises four smaller squares. (×4). Then if we look at the centre of the window, we can see another group of four squares clustered around the centre point of the 'window' (×1). Now let yourself see the window differently again and you will see a 'fat' cross shape in the centre of the window. This then divides into four smaller squares each, that all meet in the centre of the window (×4). Total: 9 squares.

Again, as with the four squares with nine smaller squares within them, in order to let ourselves see all of these possibilities we have to see areas of squares as overlapping rather than compartmentalized. We have to free our own thought. No one said that we could not have overlapping areas, or different ways of dividing up the space we see before us. Unknowingly, we often place these limitations on ourselves and cannot see any further. Part of the secret of having great thoughts is about seeing no limitations, and letting our minds free to do the rest.

Letting your mind free to see all the possibilities in the first window, will result in exactly the same number of possibilities in the second window, giving you a total of 60.

When you use this activity with your child, turn it into a game that high-lights what it is about: seeing new *possibilities*. They should not feel it is a test at all! They might want to sketch down a few copies of the windows on a piece of paper, and colour and cut out all the different possibilities, so that they can see and feel them all and how they all overlap to 'fit together' in the window. Do whichever way you decide is going to be best or appropriate for them.

Afterward, they might want to show the 'game' to their friends at school; if they do, that will be great because they will be getting a further chance to remember how, by changing and rotating their thinking, they benefited. What better kick out of the activity for them than being able to show all of their friends how to do this at school?

See how far your child gets with this activity, and if they become 'stuck' (they might not!), help them using the same method as we did for the 'Why Tree', by engaging them in a conversation, sharing knowledge, questioning and reasoning as they go along. This will enable them to get 'inside' the activity. They will come to know, and therefore remember, how they discovered the different possibilities for themselves. Enabling them to become accustomed to this process is important. With practice, when faced with an unknown prob-lem again, they will remember that by tapping into a different way of think-ing they *can* crack it.

As you progress, remember to keep their questioning and reasoning going. For example, ask them: '*What would happen if we split up the squares in this window using these two 'middle lines' here?*' (If they can't understand what you mean, you could suggest that they lightly shade in an area with a pencil to 'see' what happens.) Then continue: '*What if we did that on every side? What hap-pens?*' Help them to point out a possible group of squares, and then let them do the rest, engaging their natural questioning and reasoning as you go along.

How to help children get the best out of this activity

You could start the activity by using one window as a practice, and then letting them do the 'second window', showing you all of the possible relationships of squares *on their own*. Remember, this is not a numeracy test. The numbers 30 or 60 are immaterial in this activity. The focus here is specifically on empowering your child with the knowledge that:

◆   Thinking about problems in different ways is fun and pays off!
◆   We get to see different relationships and connections when we allow ourselves to shift and rotate our thinking.

After they have had a chance to unpack the activity for themselves, to help remind them of the power of what they have learned, it is good to consolidate by showing them the images again on page 64. They will see that unless we let ourselves see these patterns in different ways, we miss out on the opportunity to appreciate the beauty of the whole design. In the same way, Activity 2 emphasizes how thinking about the windows in at least two different ways – either as lots of separate squares, or units able to make relationships with one another in different formations – enables us to think about the problem and understand it in a different way. As soon as we do this, we can see that in any given 'problem' we encounter there may be hidden relationships within it, and that we *can* discover what these are. Thinking like this is precisely what enables us to solve problems that we have not seen before – with calm and confidence. By being able to call on this way of thinking on demand, your child knows another trick of genius that makes for great thinking. In the next chapter they will develop this to a higher level of sophistication when they learn how to apply it in a variety of problem-solving situations.

Brainbox

- ① Thinking about thinking is something great thinkers use to get great ideas.
- ① The real name for this natural mental ability is 'metacognition'.
- ① Every child has this ability, but they hardly ever get the chance to develop its fabulous potential.
- ① Being able to call on this natural thinking ability, on demand, enables our children to tackle any new problems they encounter – with calm and confidence.
- ① Letting children in on this 'trick of genius' in this chapter enables them to tap into and celebrate one of their greatest gifts – *their power to think independently.*
- ① Children are born naturally curious, they ask 'why questions' all the time.
- ① When children are given the opportunity to use this natural curiosity and thinking they can learn better and faster.
- ① Children can be taught how to do this so that it is as natural as brushing their teeth!

Chapter 5

Problem-Solving – How to Think Yourself Smarter

The problem with problem-solving

The main problem with problem solving is its name. It *sounds* difficult. If we called it 'solution-finding' it might sound a whole lot better and it would also be a more accurate description of what we are actually doing. None of us are motivated by problems as much as *finding the solutions*.

The other problem with the term 'problem-solving' is that it makes us and our children feel as if this kind of mental activity is somehow special and separate from our natural, everyday ability. Of course, problem-solving *is* a natural ability for children *and* adults! We don't call it 'problem-solving on wheels', but when our children first climb onto a bicycle, to try and learn how to ride one, that is exactly what they are doing – without even thinking about it.

'Problem-solving on wheels'
Despite the difficulties involved initially, lots of children successfully tackle the problem, 'How to ride a bicycle'. Why?

- They don't see it as a 'problem' but as an opportunity.
- They believe that it will be easy when they know how.
- They are not worried about the process, they are thinking about the *goal*.
- They can see the benefits of tackling the problem – they will be able to get from A to B by themselves – cool.
- No one ever said to them that they had to be 'super smart' to do it.
- When they fall off a couple of times and graze their knees, they are upset for five minutes and then get on with trying to succeed next time! This is because 'falling off' is not linked to 'failure', it is seen by the child as a normal process – persistence – that takes them closer to success.

Einstein did not put his success down to being particularly smart in any way. He never made any bones about the fact that it was his curiosity, combined with his persistence that contributed to his success. Einstein was not a quitter. His life had its set-backs, like all of our lives do, but he always just kept on going. He brought this same persistence to his work and the cracking of abstract problems.

Abstract problem-solving is something we do mostly in our heads; it doesn't involve us in any more *physical* activity than using pen and paper! But whether you are problem-solving in a practical situation, or doing it all in your head, it doesn't matter. In order to 'crack' a problem we have to apply our thinking to a problem and stay with it, otherwise we won't find a solution.

Children everywhere have stayed with the problem of how to ride a bicycle until they succeeded. Children, like Einstein, focus on mastering the art of solution-finding when faced with a bicycle for the first time. The only difference between the two is that Einstein mastered the art of solution-finding at his desk. Your child solves bicycle riding whilst tearing around at high speed on two wobbly wheels instead! You decide which is more complex to do!

Your child can learn how to master the art of solution-finding in less physical, more abstract situations than riding a bicycle. After doing the activities in this chapter they will see that all problem-solving activities, in whatever guise they present themselves in, for what they all really are: *an opportunity to show people how smart they are!*

For younger children, who have recently started junior school, preconceptions about problem-solving questions may not be an issue, and they will enter the activities in this chapter with fresh eyes. Children further on in their school career may hold some preconceptions which, depending upon their experiences may or may not be positive. That's fine! This chapter is designed to unravel any mysteries about problem-solving and show them all the tricks they need so that from whichever point your child starts, by the end of it they will see their abilities shine through. Each of the activities has been designed so that in the future, whenever your child hears 'problem-solving', they will automatically put it through a 'thought switch' and think: *'Right, yeah, I know what this is! This is an opportunity to 'solution-find'! And I can do that!'*

Getting to grips with problem-solving

Worldwide, there are a number of myths that have traditionally surrounded problem-solving. So the first thing we need to do is to clear the path for straight thinking here by debunking those myths. The FAQ section below separates the fact from the fiction.

FAQs

 Q: Are pen-and-paper type problem-solving activities more difficult than practical kinds?

A: No! Same principle, just a different context. Practical problem-solving in everyday life typically involves us in finding out about tangible relationships between parts of a problem we can see and touch. For example, presented with riding a bike for the first time involves us figuring out how best to position our hands on the handlebars, and our feet on the pedals, in relation to achieving our goal – keeping our balance on the bike so that we can ride it. *Abstract* problem-solving typically involves us using *intangible* relationships between the parts of a problem to reach our goal. That means we rely more on being able to juggle a problem around in our heads, rather than in our hands, to find the solutions. But whether a problem is intangible or tangible we can still crack it. It is just that we often have more practice, and therefore more confidence dealing with tangible problems in real life.

The most important point your child needs to know and remember is that whenever we encounter a problem for the first time, no matter what it is, our minds are busy:

★   Establishing relationships between things;
★   Finding solutions.

Q: Is problem-solving something that is going to benefit our children in particular subject areas, such as mathematics, for example?

A: No! This is one of the biggest myths of all! Finding relationships between things to solve problems and find solutions are useful skills in mathematics, but they are not mental activities unique to this subject. If you look at the few 'missions impossible' that we and our children do in the course of a day or week, you can see that problem-solving is a fact of life – whatever we are doing.

- ◆ 'How am I going to beat the city rush hour tonight, so that I can pick my child up from school on time?'
- ◆ 'How can I go to that party on Saturday night and still have time to do my history essay for Monday?'
- ◆ 'How can I get Dad to buy me a new pair of those designer jeans, even though I only just had my birthday present?'
- ◆ 'How can I impress the panel in my interview?'

You could say that life is one big problem-solving activity! The aim of this chapter is for your child to be able to see that they *already* have the ability to solve problems. It's a natural human ability. So all problem-solving activities, wherever they come across them, are something they can do. But by learning a few 'tricks of genius' they will be able to unlock and maximize upon their natural gift whenever they need to.

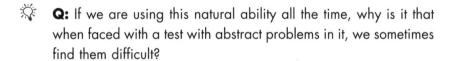

Q: If we are using this natural ability all the time, why is it that when faced with a test with abstract problems in it, we sometimes find them difficult?

A: To put it simply, the context throws us. Our first challenge therefore is to 'find a way' into the problem. Unless we train ourselves not to let the situation throw us, we may panic at this stage. This is because the parts of the problem we see on a piece of paper in front of us can seem totally alien to us. *Seem* is the word to remember! The problem may look alien, but that does not mean that your child lacks the skills, knowledge and experience to solve it! The trick is being able to *transfer* what they already know to the 'strange' situation they are looking at. The activities in this chapter show children how to do this effectively and to succeed.

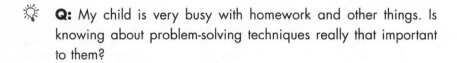

Q: My child is very busy with homework and other things. Is knowing about problem-solving techniques really that important to them?

A: Yes! Remember in the global knowledge economy, developing individual thinking and creativity is a key skill for children in the 21st century. Problem-solving questions frequently feature on ability tests used in education internationally (*see* chapter 2), precisely because they test *thinking* as opposed to just how much our child knows. Have no fear! The friendly activities gently and effectively provide your child with a range of top tips and tricks to use in these tests. They will be able to approach abstract problem-solving questions from an informed and skilled vantage point.

Solution-finding made easy

Everything is easy when you know how. Strategy is all important in teaching our children to be better 'solution-finders' when they are faced with a problem-solving question. But 'strategy' is just a term. It doesn't mean anything to a child until they feel the power of using one. In order for them to get the best benefit from the activities in this chapter they therefore need to learn the 'tricks of the trade' by actually using them in *practice*.

6 Steps to smarter thinking in problem-solving

The 6 Steps below are for *your* eyes only – for *the moment*. Why? If you just *told* your child the 6 Steps, straight out of the blue, without them having any experience of doing them in practice, they might remember a few words, but that is all. The steps would not be alive in their minds. What we want are smart strategies in words, turned into smart thoughts they can use! The only way to make this happen is for them to learn the 6 Steps by *doing* them. That way, they make the 6 Steps their own, to use again and again, whenever they want or need to.

After they have done the activities in this chapter, you can then either run through these 6 Steps with them, focusing on the 'top tips', or if you think it is more appropriate, let them do this for themselves. Either way they get double the benefit.

- *After* they have learned the thinking strategies for themselves doing the activities, reading through the 6 Steps serves as an excellent way to round off their learning. They provide a summary of top tricks and tips for your child.
- *Any* time your child needs to revise this topic, the 6 Steps, combined with their memory of actually doing the activities here, will provide them with a quick reference booster.

So here are the 6 Steps (for your eyes only for the moment):

1 Remember to see all 'problems' as opportunities to find solutions.

Immediately, thinking in this way does two things in our minds:

★   We set off to find the solution;
★   Finding the solution becomes the only focus of our concentration.

This is important because our mind *expects* to be able to solve whatever it is. Our minds are now thinking: '*This has a solution. What is it? How can I find it?*', rather than: '*This is a problem and I don't know the answer.*' The big difference in thinking here means an even bigger benefit – quicker solution-finding!

2 Consciously focus on putting your thinking to work.

Thinking about problems *subconsciously* is what all of us do, including our children, whenever we are presented with an unfamiliar situation. As seen earlier, we do this automatically when figuring out how to ride a bicycle. But in the middle of an examination hall, faced with imposed silence, a ticking clock, pen, paper and an abstract problem in a sterile test, we can sometimes feel like rabbits in headlights. We panic! This has more to do with the context of the problem (the tense examination room) than our ability to solve what we find in front of us. It is important that your child remembers this, so that when they are faced with such a situation they remember to flip their focus: forget the context and instead *consciously* apply their thinking power to the problem and winning!

3 Find hidden relationships by thinking 'outside' of the problem.

In abstract problem-solving questions found in ability tests, this is a particularly important strategy. Children have to think 'outside' of the problem to find the solution. This is because typical abstract problem-solving questions used in these kinds of tests do not *give* the relationships between the elements in a problem. That is the bit they are asking the candidate to come up with! To find those relationships your child has to use their own thinking and ideas.

4 Strike a balance between applying what you already know and keeping your mind open to new possibilities.

One strategy in problem-solving is to transfer what we already know to a new situation in order to help us solve it. Another strategy is to keep our

Top tip: the 3Rs of problem-solving – relax, rattle and roll!

When faced with a problem in an exam, free up your thinking by saying to yourself: 'Relax, Rattle and Roll!' This will help you to *relax* yourself and remember that the key to great solution-finding is to:

★   Let yourself see the problem in different ways (*rattling!*);
★   Keep rattling your thoughts around until you find the solution (*rolling!*).

Think of a newborn baby when you first give it a toy. It grabs hold of it and starts exploring it. It shakes it around to see if anything happens. It rolls it around a bit on the floor and tries to 'gum it to death' with its mouth. The baby, in a relaxed, easy state, is getting to know about the new toy by 'rattling and rolling' it to see what it does and how it does it. As adults we get a bit more sophisticated about how we tackle new situations – well, most of the time! But at the same time when faced with a new situation we have a tendency not to relax but to get uptight instead. As a result, we lose the relaxed way in which a baby lets itself 'rattle and roll'. Whether we are a baby or an adult, great thinking is more likely to occur when we are in a relaxed state and let our thinking flow. So remind children to let themselves relax, rattle and roll, and they will find the solution.

Top tip: the answer's hidden in your head!

Remember, you have all the answers in your head. Tap into your own thoughts and ideas to find the relationships between the different parts of a problem, and you have then mastered the art of solution-finding.

Think about it this way. The tester knows what these relationships are and so can you. If, of course, you remember to relax, rattle and roll and to ask yourself these questions:

★   *'How can I make these bits of the problem relate to each other?'*
★   *'What do I already know that I can use here?'*
★   *'When have I seen a something like this before?'*
★   *'What did I do to solve it?'*
★   *'How can I think about this in another way?'*

By learning to use these kinds of questions children consciously begin to apply and tap into their natural metacognitive ability to 'solution-find'. Remember, metacognition is that big word with a simple meaning: 'thinking about thinking'. It is our mind's ability to keep adapting its thinking to solve new problems or deal with situations. When your child is problem-solving they use this ability without knowing it. Using the strategies here, they are learning how to *maximize* upon the power of this natural ability.

mind open to exploring new possibilities. The essential trick your child needs to know and remember is that good problem-solving technique strikes a balance between using *both* of these strategies.

Research indicates that ordinarily we are creatures of habit. We have a tendency toward using what we already know before we look for new possibilities. What do I mean? How does this work in practice? The following case study provides a practical example.

How to give yourself grey hairs – instantly!

A few years ago I decided to buy an automatic car for the first time. Before then, my experience of driving had been using gears. Anyone who has made this switch from using gears to an automatic will know what happened next. The car was all gleaming and brand new. It was a lovely day. I was happy. I drove off down the road from the car showroom enjoying my new vehicle, when I had to slow down behind a car. My mind did not see 'slowing down' as some sort of problem-solving activity that I had to think about. I had slowed down countless times *before* when I was driving a car, so it would be the same here. Wrong! I didn't just slow down. I hit the emergency brake with my left foot, causing my car to 'kangaroo' to a stop, my passenger to go quite pale, and myself to sprout grey hairs.

Why did this happen? My past experience of the activity 'driving a car' had put me in a mindset that had conditioned me to think that when 'slowing down' I needed to use both feet – my left foot on the clutch and my right foot on the accelerator – otherwise the car would stall. In the new situation, what my left foot hit when it reached out was now no longer the clutch, it was the emergency break for the automatic. Some of my past knowledge and experience was useful, such as: 'when driving a car I use my feet to slow down'. But I also had to let go some of my previous experience of driving cars. It was preventing me from finding a solution to the existing situation. I needed to stop thinking about using two feet for breaking and start using just one. My passenger just needed to get out of the car!

Of course, I was not dealing with a pen-and-paper problem-solving activity. But the principle is the same. To be successful in my new situation I had to strike a balance between using what I already knew and opening my mind to new possibilities.

5 Remain calm and confident.

Whatever the problem, no matter how 'weird' it looks, keep calm and remember that you have the ability to solve it – whatever it is. When children remember this they are unstoppable!

6 Hold this thought: There is always a solution.

Belief is everything in problem-solving. If we expect success, we will achieve it. Knowledge really is power here. Children stand a better chance at succeeding on problem-solving questions if they have a range of thinking strategies which they can apply. They enter any new problem-solving situation confident in the knowledge that *they can crack it*!

Top tip: strike a balance

When you are solution-finding, always take charge of your own thinking. Use what you already know, but remember to keep your mind open to new ways of thinking about things.

Let the games commence!

The 6 Steps have shown *you* what is possible for your child. By doing the activities *your child* can discover and come to know these smarter ways of thinking – for themselves!

The range of 'problems' that your child experiences in the following activities are specifically designed to do four things:

1   Dismiss any mystique about problem-solving by showing them *what to look for* when they are in full-blown solution-finding mode.
2   Let them see and experience that problem-solving questions can appear in many guises, but are based on similar tricks.
3   Develop key thinking strategies in solution-finding.
4   Have fun at the same time!

The more 'guises' children see problem-solving appearing in, the less mysterious the whole thing becomes. We have already seen how riding a bicycle for the first time is literally 'problem-solving on wheels'. The activities below continue to develop this idea of diversity in problem-solving by introducing them to some less physical and more conceptual types of problem-solving activities. In particular, the activities focus on taking the sting out of abstract problem-solving questions of the type that appear in ability and IQ tests. Such questions have less to do with knowledge and more with ways of thinking.

By practising the thinking strategies in the activities in this chapter your child will be toning up their mental problem-solving abilities. This will put them in excellent stead for 'solution-finding', whenever they encounter abstract problem-solving questions, whether at school or beyond in their individual careers. At the same time, your child is learning another 'trick of genius': how to capitalize *consciously* on their own natural problem-solving ability. Let's get started!

Activity 3: The Four Riddles

The Four Riddles shows your child one guise in which problem-solving activity can arise. This activity:

♦ Sets the tone for the rest of the activities by using a fun and 'friendly face' to introduce them to this topic;

♦ Enables your child to see how making relationships between bits of information helps them solution-find;

♦ Highlights the fact that relationship finding is a key strategy in solution-finding;

♦ Provides a mental warm-up for the activities that follow.

Why riddles? For children, riddles are like learning how to ride a bike; they do them without 'thinking' about them. Probably because they have never seen something like this in a test, they do not associate riddles with thinking activity. But just like learning how to ride a bicycle, riddles engage children in a *great deal* of thinking activity!

How to help children get the best out of this activity

Introduce the activity to them, not as a problem-solving exercise, but simply as 'Four Riddles'. Then let them choose whether you start by reading the riddles out or letting them read them for themselves. Next, let them guess each one. If they get stuck, as with the activities in chapter 4, let *them* figure it out. This is an important part of developing their own problem-solving ability. The only time you need to give information directly to them here is if they have not come across a word before and need to know what it means. That's fine. By mixing a bit of knowledge sharing with a few questions, you guide them in the right direction and, importantly, they will be able to arrive at their destination for *themselves*. (The answers to the riddles are given at the end of the chapter.)

RIDDLE 1: 'NO ROSES IN MY CHEEKS'

I fall but land gently,
I do not crash.
My beauty is cold,
No roses in my cheeks.
Only delicate white lace,
Knitted together like frost.
Children catch me in their warm hands,
And when they do, I'm suddenly lost!

What am I?

RIDDLE 2: 'THEY FOLLOW THE SUN'

My face is golden,
But my heart is dark bronze,
My neck long and thin,
My head overly large.
My hands draped in green,
They follow the sun,
My body follows too,
But my feet, they stay put,
They are not made to run.

What am I?

RIDDLE 3: 'MY SKIN NEVER AGES'.

My skin never ages,
I am 80, yet in full bloom!
My clothing is oily,
Yet I am perfectly dry.
My eyes can wander,
But I cannot move.

I long for a cleaning,
Only a dusting if you mind.
I am far too delicate for polish,
– Would you be so kind?

What am I?

RIDDLE 4: 'PEARLS ARE MY HALLS'.

I am a home abandoned
Pearls are my halls,
Turquoise is my view.
Beige is my carpet.
Sometimes all is smooth silence
Then everything is roughly crashed
Cup me to your ear,
And gentle sounds you will hear.
– If you can find me in one piece.

What am I?

'Think Time' for Children: learning to think from reflections.

After you have praised them for working them all out, make a time-out sign with your hands, as though on a sports pitch and get them to do this with you. This is the signal for 'think time' and it is valuable that they do this. Ask your child to reflect for a moment. They need to backtrack on what they just did to arrive at the answers. This can be done by means of a casual conversation, prompting them with the following kinds of questions:

♦   *'What was the first thing that came into your mind?'*

♦   'How did you find the answer?'
♦   'What were the clues that helped you?'
♦   'How did you fit all the different clues together?'
♦   'When did you feel sure that you had guessed it?'

Reflection is an important part of good problem-solving technique. After each of the activities in this chapter your child has an opportunity to do this for themselves. Taking time out to reflect on what they have done is an important part of developing good problem-solving strategies. It enables children to:

♦   Unpack the strategy they used to find a solution;
♦   Think if there is anything they could have done to arrive at the solution better and/or quicker;
♦   Think what things did not work, and what they could do differently next time.
♦   Think what strategies worked well for them and why.

In this activity we were only looking at riddles. But the ability to reflect is a thinking strategy that can help children to improve their technique in problem-solving, no matter the complexity of the problem. It wouldn't matter if we had just successfully constructed a new bridge, made a scientific discovery or climbed a mountain face. In other words, reflecting on their problem-solving strategies is a lifelong skill they can keep benefiting from again and again.

CHECKPOINT

Q: What is the main benefit of this reflection for my child in the context of the Four Riddles?

A: By thinking about what they did here, your child will come to see a natural ability that they can use in solution-finding: making con-

nections between a diverse range of clues. They will be able to unpack their own thinking process and see *how* they were able to make the relationships they did, even though what they read or listened to at first seemed totally unconnected. They were able to take all the clues and bring them together to find a solution – the object they all described. To discover this for themselves is magical, but until someone points out that they have this ability they are not consciously aware of how powerful their thinking can be.

Before you move on to the next activity, check that they have fully grasped that making relationships between things is the key to the art of solution-finding. Remember from the 6 Steps that this is also a major part of effective problem-solving, so they cannot afford to move on without it. The following activity helps them make this knowledge their own by switching their role from solution-finder to riddle-maker.

Activity 4: I'm the Riddle-maker!

When they have finished their reflection on Activity 3, let your child in on the reverse of solution-finding – problem-making! Ask them to choose something, an orange, a household pet, a landmark, a clock, for example, keep it to themselves and make a riddle up of their own about it. When they have done this you, another adult, friend or sibling then has to guess the answer.

Switching the tables from being a 'solution-finder' to 'problem setter', is a practical way of letting children experience the importance of making connections and relationships between things in solution-finding. Trying to set problems for themselves helps them to internalize this idea. They will see that in making a riddle, they have to think up clues, using a wide range of ideas and associations that all point to one thing – the object of the riddle.

Giving problems a human face

At the same time, your child will see that if they make the connections *too* obvious then it won't be a riddle any more! And this is precisely what examiners do when they are making up questions in ability tests. They can only give so many clues, otherwise it is no longer a test. In a gentle way, Activity 4 also acts to remove the mystique associated with puzzles, riddles and problems-solving questions in test papers, by giving these things a human face. It shows your child that all puzzles, tests, examinations, etc. originate from someone's head! Why is that important knowledge for children? When a child is presented with a puzzle or problem-solving question on a test paper they cannot visualize its origins, they do not know who created it, they cannot picture a person in their head. It is as if the problem just landed on the paper in front of them. So whenever they see a problem-solving activity on a test paper or in a magazine, they have a mysterious, almost 'Men in Black' image associated with its creators! In doing this activity, once your child has had a go at creating a problem and testing other people *for themselves*, they will find that:

◆   All problems are mortal;
◆   They are created by ordinary people;
◆   They can therefore be solved by ordinary people!

End of mystery. It will be a bit like when they discovered the 'tooth fairy' was really Mum, only less upsetting!

Activity 5: Solution-Finding Fun I – 5 Tricks of Genius

Now we are going to move up a gear. Activity 5 takes the types of questions found in ability tests, and purposely presents them to your child in a fun format. A quick flip on to Activity 6: Solution-Finding Fun II (see page 96), and you will see that the problems there take on a more formal guise. The idea is that once children have learned the '5 tricks' they used to find solutions in Activity 5, they will see in Activity 6 that formal problem-solving questions are just as simple to solve when they have a few 'tricks of the trade' up their sleeve!

How to help children get the best out of this activity

Introduce Activity 5 to them as a solution-finding game. Remember the message for children here is that these are not 'problems'. They are just great *opportunities* to do some solution-finding!

This activity enables them to build upon, and apply at a more sophisticated level, what they have already learned – *that finding relationships between things finds solutions*. They are also going to learn and apply three thinking strategies from the 6 Steps, by learning how to:

★   Find solutions by striking a balance between using what they already know and keeping their minds open to new possibilities;
★   Use the 3Rs of problem-solving: Relax, Rattle and Roll their thinking to free their ideas up and find the solution;
★   Consciously focus their thinking.

The last point sees this activity developing your child's natural metacognitive abilities in the problem-solving process: consciously adapting their thinking strategy until they come up with the solution. As you now know, most of the time our children do this thinking subconsciously, but here your child is learning how to really maximize on this natural mental power and apply it in problem-solving questions.

Remember to let your child figure out the solutions to all the activities for *themselves*, using the 3Rs. To get them started, rattling and rolling their

Solution-Finding Fun 1

a)

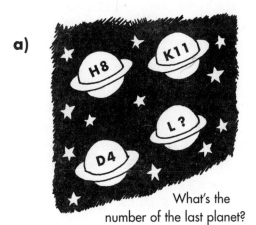

What's the
number of the last planet?

b)

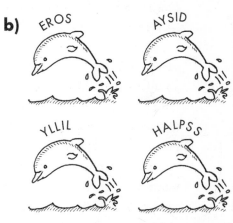

Which is the odd one out?

c)

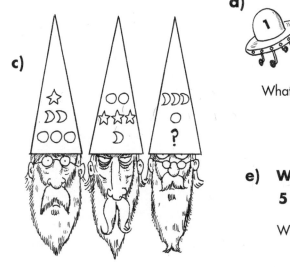

What comes next?
a) ◯ ◯   b) 𝔇𝔇𝔇   c) ☆☆   d) ◯

d)

What comes next?

e) **WANT**   **GRIN**   _ _ _
      5 2 4 1   **3 6 7 4**   **5 7 4**

What's the missing word?

ideas and thoughts, use the starter questions provided for each activity. As they do each activity, your child will learn 5 Tricks of Genius that they can use when they are faced with other abstract problems used on ability-type tests.

a) PLANETS

To solve this problem, children need to change letters into numbers, using the alphabet. Here is a helpful starter question for your child: '*How can we turn letters into numbers?*' Let them try to think this through for themselves first. If they can't quite figure it, ask them: '*How many letters are there in the alphabet?*' (Answer: 26). Then let them see the table below. So if D was a number of the alphabet what number would it be? (Answer: D4 – one of planet's names). Then let your child do the rest. Even if they got the answer right away, it is a good idea for them to see the whole of the table just to help them remember the trick for future reference.

A	1	N	14
B	2	O	15
C	3	P	16
D	4	Q	17
E	5	R	18
F	6	S	19
G	7	T	20
H	8	U	21
I	9	V	22
J	10	W	23
K	11	X	24
L	12	Y	25
M	13	Z	26

[Answer: the missing number of the last planet is 12]

b) DOLPHINS

Helpful starter question for your child: *'What would happen if we changed the order of the letters in these words? Let's start with 'EROS'; what other word could that make?'* Then let your child rattle and roll each of the words until they find the odd word out.

[**Answer: except for Splash (Halpss) all the jumbled words above the dolphins are names of flowers: Rose, Daisy, Lilly.**]

c) WIZARDS

There are three different types of shape in the wizard's hats – stars, crescents and circles. Now cast your eyes from the top to the bottom of each hat, and then left to right across the rows of shapes in each hat. You will see that either way you view them, there's always 1, 2 or 3 circles, crescents and stars, not in any particular order. Helpful starter questions for your child: *'How many times do crescents of moon appear in each of the wizard hats?'* *'How many times do circles appear in each of the wizard hats?'* *'How many times do stars appear in each of the wizard hats?'* *'So what's missing?'*

[**Answer: c – two stars**]

d) ALIENS

This is a case of finding out what we do to the first number to get to the second number. For example, it might be a case of subtracting, adding or multiplying the number 3. Helpful starter question for your child: *'What number could we add to 1 to make 5?'*

[**Answer: 13**]

The example has purposely used addition and small numbers so as to be accessible to younger as well as older children. Which numbers are used is not important – learning the trick is. If your child is older and wants more of a challenge on this question, then ask them to devise a sequence pattern of their own. For example, you could have a sequence of 2, 3, 8, 63 …? Each time the first number is multiplied by itself (squared) and then you take away 1 to get the next number. So the answer is: $(63 \times 63) - 1 = 3,968$.

e) CODE CRACKER

The trick here is to see which numbers are associated with which letters in the words. When you do that you can then use the number clues to spell out the missing word. This is another ploy sometimes used in ability tests. Children can see that code cracking is easy once they know how to use the clues they are given to find the solution. By doing this activity soon after they did activity (a) (in which they used a different trick to change letters into numbers), your child will also learn one of the 6 Steps to smarter thinking: to strike a balance between using what they already have learned, and keeping their mind open to new possibilities.

Helpful starter questions: '*What letter was 5 connected to, in the first word?*' '*And what letter was 7 connected to?*' And so on, until they crack it!

[**Answer: Win**]

At the end of this activity your child will have been doing a lot of mental 'rattling and rolling'! So, time to take 'time out' for reflection. Let them backtrack, think about what they did, and unpack and discuss whichever of the 5 Tricks of Genius they used in each case to arrive at the solution.

Planting the seeds of success

As they solve these abstract problems it can be helpful to use the remaining top tips given in the 6 Steps to help plant seeds of success in your child's mind as they work out the answers. For example:

◆   *'Remember, there is **always** a solution! You know the answer is hidden in your head! You* can *do it!'*

Einstein did it too!

What do you do when your child is putting forward good ideas, but they are not necessarily the appropriate ones? When your child tries these activities for the first time, they may not always get to the answer straight away. That's perfectly fine! Neither did Einstein! And *they* need to know that!

For Einstein to achieve his solution-finding it took staying power as well as mental power. Remind your child about that, and what Einstein put his problem-solving ability down to from his 'genius' standpoint: persistence! Remind them too of the analogy of learning to ride a bicycle; they accept falling off a bicycle as something that is likely to happen when they first start trying to master it; the same applies here! The Japanese have a wonderful proverb about success: 'Fall down seven. Stand up eight'. Share this proverb with children and the message is clear: trying and succeeding go hand in hand. With a few smart tricks they will easily rocket through these activities.

Activity 6: Solution-Finding Fun II – 5 Tricks of Genius

If children are doing this straight after Activity 5, everything will be fresh in their heads. If not, and it has been some time since you and your child did the last activity, that's fine too, as long as they get a chance for a quick booster session going through the activities and answers in Activity 5 again, they will be ready to go again!

Now, using the 5 Tricks of Genius they learned in Activity 5, it is time for them to relax, rattle and roll their way through the next set of activities.

Solution-Finding Fun II

a) What is the missing word?

8 + 5 + 1 + 18 + 20 = HEART
2 + 5 + 1 + 20 = _ _ _ _

b) Which is the odd one out?

EPESH
REHOS
RETIG
BIRBAT

c) What comes next?

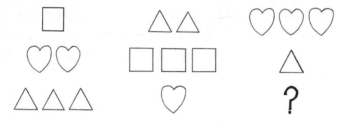

d) What comes next?

1, 6, 11, _

e) What's the missing word?

MARS   KITE   _ _ _ _ _
4 1 7 8   6 5 2 9   8 4 1 7 2

To save time, for question (a), let them see and use the alphabetical numbers table given earlier (see page 92). By letting them look at this again as they are doing the activity, it locks the trick into their memory. Now all *you* have to do is to watch your child puff up with pride at just how smart they are! The answers are given below.

Answers to Solution-Finding Fun II:

a) BEAT (using the alphabet to turn numbers into letters).

b) TIGER (all other words when unscrambled are names of animals that do not hunt prey for food: Sheep, Horse, Rabbit).

c) b: two squares (this completes the pattern, the square shapes are the only ones without a pair in them so that is the answer).

d) 16 (add 5 to each number to make the next one).

e) SMART (the letters in each of the words MARS and KITE each have a 'code' number – using these clues cracks the code to get the answer).

The cool-down

When they have done all of the activities in this part of the chapter your child will have done a thorough thinking workout! So now they need a thorough thinking 'cool-down' too. Congratulate them on doing a great job. Then call a 'timeout' to give them some thinking time to ask themselves questions such as:

◆   'What did I do to find the solution in each one?'
◆   'What were the tricks I used?'

Then share with them, or let them read for themselves, the summary given below of the different techniques and strategies they used. It is written in the first person so that when children read it for themselves they can make what they did their own, by personalizing the tricks. Plus it rounds off the activity by having the chance to say how brilliant they are!

Summary: 5 Tricks of Genius for Solution-Finding!

♦   'I changed letters into numbers using the alphabet (jammy!).'
♦   'I learned how to crack letter and number codes (wicked!).'
♦   'I played with jumbled up words to find ones that made sense (easy!).'
♦   'I looked for patterns with shapes; I could see what was next (clever!).'
♦   'I found patterns in numbers, so I knew what was next (smart!).'
♦   'I relaxed, 'rattled' and 'rolled' my way to the solution!'
♦   'I found links between anything and everything!'
♦   'Why? 'Cos I'm a clever cat - and modest too!'

The 6 Steps - live and kicking

After your child has had time to reflect on the summary above, and to cool down from doing the activities, show them, or read through with them, the 6 Steps that began this chapter. Having done all the activities for real, the 6 Steps will now come alive in your child's mind. Mission accomplished! Any time they need to refresh their solution-finding skills, they will be able to go back to both the 6 Steps and the 5 Tricks of Genius summary above.

The tricks they have learned and used to crack the problems in the activities here, have provided them with a grounding in how to tackle the types of questions found in ability and IQ tests used the world over. Your child now knows the types of relationships between things that testers use in setting problems, and therefore what to look for to find the solutions. Of course, the actual problems presented in tests are going to be many and varied. So ideally, the activities they have done here are best followed up by providing them with regular opportunities to practice, in different contexts and situations, the problem-solving tricks they have now learned – and look out for new ones too! The 'Where can I get information on …?' section at the end of this book shows you where you can find sample tests as well as fun, problem-solving activities.

With the 6 Steps your child has discovered the best trick of all – their ability to think. The tricks they have learned here may not directly solve every problem for them in every test, but something else *will* – their mind! Your child has learned something that Einstein and other great thinkers before him have always known: *when we learn to think, all problems become 'solvable'*.

CHECKPOINT

Q: I have seen some ability tests which use questions like:

Bird is to seed as squirrel is to ………? [fish; nut; hedgehog; rabbit]

Would my child still be able to use the strategies they have learned here to solve these kinds of 'problems'?

A: Yes. In order to find a solution here, your child is still looking for a *relationship between* the different elements in the problem. In this case the relationship is something an animal eats. Birds eat seeds. So the answer is 'nuts'. Of course, squirrels could eat a whole range of other things apart from nuts, as could a bird. The tester knows that. But the logic of the relationship is what is being asked of the child in this case, not how many different kinds of foods a bird or squirrel eats. The most logical answer from the choices given is 'nut'.

What would happen, though, if the words used in this kind of problem were suddenly changed to:

Radius is to arm as occiput is to ....? [shoulder; foot; skull; knee]

You may or may not know the answer is 'skull'. The relationship is bones in different parts of the body. The radius is a bone in the lower part of the arm, the occipital bone is found at the back of the skull. But unless we were experts in human physiology, or had a good dictionary to hand, we would not be able to solve this. That is the difference between problem-solving questions which are *really* testing our children's *thinking* ability – like the ones your child has done in this chapter, and those which are testing general knowledge.

As a parent, this is an important point to remember about any kind of ability test your child may undertake. Find out what it is *really* testing. What does it *really* tell you about your child's ability? Top tips for finding out about tests are given in chapter 2, but if you dived straight into this section of the book and have not read this yet, then a quick flick back will give you the low-down.

What about computer games?

Do computer games help our children sharpen their thinking skills? This is one of the 'great debates' in children's learning at the moment. Here is the answer in a nutshell: it depends on the game. There are some good strategy games which do involve children thinking through problems and devising solutions for themselves. The games that benefit them do not just take them through an entertaining, but static, learning loop, in which they learn a couple of simple moves and strategies early on in the game, and then proceed to repeat 1000 times until they 'reach level 720', where they do more of the same! A scenario for this kind of game goes something like this. They start off learning to swat monsters, before the monsters 'get them' at level one. By the time they progress to level 3 the monsters have got bigger, but your child is still doing the same thing: swatting monsters. If it were not for the graphics and speed at which this repeated activity took place your child would probably fall asleep at the first level – out of sheer boredom! In this kind of game, no problem-solving or thinking is required, just lots of adrenalin to keep up with the speed at which players robotically swat monsters!

Whether you adore them or loathe them, these games are here to stay and it is good to keep checking out what new kinds of products are available. Since computer games first became popular, games developers have looked to produce products that interest children and adults enough to challenge and keep our attention. This is after all the essence of all good gaming whether on a computer screen or in a traditional board game: pitting our wits against situations and competitors. As children get used to the older computer game products they are looking for new challenges. This is a rapidly evolving and developing area. Products do vary and depending upon the game, your child may have both an entertaining and intellectually challenging experience. The trick is to know how to get value for money, by knowing what to look for on the packet. Here's a checklist you can use if you decide to go shopping for one.

Checklist: 'gaming'

✓   **Q:** *What is the precise objective of the game?*

✓   **A:** This is usually summarized on the back of the packet. Cut through the 'hype' about how exciting the game is going to be and look to find out what the objective is. This will give you a good indication of the kind of thinking or no thinking your child is going to be involved in!

✓   **Q:** *Does it have any particular educational value? Do they learn anything?*

✓   **A:** It is worth scouring the blurb to see if you hold in your hands one of those games that actually teaches your child something as a spin-off. In which case, success in the game will not just be dependent on quick reflexes and learning a few moves, but also upon them having to learn something about a topic that they can use in school work.

✓   **Q:** *Does it mention the words 'problem-solving'?*

✓   **A:** Gradually some products have begun to appear which mix problem-solving types of activities with multimedia graphics and this is to be welcomed. The message here though is, don't be blinded by science! Good graphics may look exciting and sell the product because they are attractive. Check out on the packet for what else it does for your child apart from look great!

✓   **Q:** *Could I get better value here by buying my child a 'traditional' game?*

✓   **A:** There are plenty of traditional games that help our children think. Chess is an absolute classic that is brilliant for developing thinking skills! Whether played virtually on a computer or using the real life chess board and pieces. Some of these now come in beautifully imaginative designs to capture the imagination and they can make playing chess a real family event. So, if your shopping expedition is unfruitful any day in the computer store, check out the more traditional gaming sections in other stores and you might find, or rediscover some traditional gems that are fun and great for your child's thinking too.

Brainbox

- ① Problem-solving is a natural human ability – we all do it!
- ① Great thinkers maximize upon this ability.
- ① The label 'problem-solving' can mask for children what these questions are really about – solution-finding!
- ① When a child first rides a bicycle they are 'solution-finding' – on wheels!
- ① Whether learning to ride a bicycle for the first time or doing a problem-solving question in a test paper – your child is still doing the same thing: trying to figure out the solution.
- ① Children can master bicycle riding because they know what to look out for.
- ① Children can master problem-solving questions on ability and IQ tests too, when they know what to look for – *relationships* between items.
- ① The 'trick of genius' is for your child to be aware of what these relationships are, and how to detect them.
- ① The 6 Steps, combined with the activities in this chapter, show your child how to do just that.
- ① What they learn here, your child can use forever: problems can be cracked and 'solution-finding' *can* be fun! – When you know how.

Flexing their thinking muscles with problem-solving activities will hone your child's natural thinking ability. But you may have noticed as you read through this chapter, and your child did the activities, that all the problems they encountered were 'close-ended'. This means that the answers to all the problems were pre-set and therefore consisted of one solution. In real life, we all know that there are in fact many problems to be solved, each with possibilities for many different kinds of solutions. When someone comes up with an invention to sort a real life problem out, we hail them a genius. No one pre-set the solutions or the problems that these 'geniuses' tackled. So how did they come up with their brilliant solution? Answer: they were using another natural ability our children possess. It is something that cannot be captured and bottled by a test with problem-solving questions on it. Something that fascinates us, is magical in every way and which our children are bursting with – *creativity*!

In this chapter, your child learned that a 'trick of genius' in problem-solving was to keep their mind open to explore new possibilities. In chapter 6 your child will see the benefits for themselves of exploring new possibilities on a much wider scale. They will learn how to fly at a higher level of thinking, and how to unlock their own special gift of creativity – so prepare for lift off.

[Answers to Riddles: 1) Snow Flake; 2) Sunflower; 3) Oil painting; 4) Sea shell.]

Chapter 6

Lift off! Unlocking the Gift of Creativity

The 'wow' factor

When people make a new discovery, create a great new design or invent something that benefits many people, we are all wowed and hail them a genius! The question on everybody's lips is: '*How did they do it?*' Thinking creatively played a great part in how these people achieved what they did. As we saw in section I, no one knows for certain where creativity in any one person begins or ends. However, what we do know is that whatever else creativity may be, we can see it at play every day. Where? In our children of course!

So, if all children have this gift of creativity, why is it that they don't all go on to make fantastic discoveries? As we grow older, unless we learn to nurture and value our creativity, we don't lose it, as much as we get out of practice. It is still there, deep inside us, but unless our careers and/or leisure activities regularly engage our own individual creativity, our ability to tap into it with the same carefree abandon we once did as children becomes swamped by other concerns. If you have ever challenged yourself to do something new and different, such as study a new language, begin your own business, or anything that takes you out of your normal situation, you will have experienced that buzz you get from freeing up your mind's creativity.

Thinking and creativity

What patterns of thought kick in when we are thinking creatively? In the last chapter, all the problems your child solved were about deducting pre-set, close-ended solutions. Initially they used some aspects of creative thinking (rattling and rolling), but once they had learned the tricks of how to crack the problems, less creative thinking was required. Learning how to 'rattle and roll' problems formed a good foundation for them to begin to unleash their creative thinking abilities. But now, the activities in this chapter focus on showing your child how to lift the lid off of their thinking and *really* think creatively about things. They will learn how to think at a higher level.

Creative thinking gets into top gear when there is no pre-set solution. It happens when a person is thinking about an open-ended question or problem. For instance, how to design a new kind of car engine is a typically open-ended problem – to find solutions we would have to think critically about the drawbacks of current designs for car engines, then use a combination of our own knowledge and ideas to come up with new types of car engines. Creative thinking involves children tapping into:

★   Thinking critically;
★   Using existing knowledge;
★   Exploring new ways of thinking.

By doing this, they begin to think at a *higher level* about any given topic or subject, and their minds bounce ideas around. In the process they are opening their mind to the possibility of coming up with something new and original. Result – creative thinking.

What starts a person off thinking like this in the first place? Have you ever been to a supermarket and struggled with a wobbly trolley around the aisles and thought: '*This is daft. Can't they come up with anything better?*' As soon as we start to think critically about something like this, we begin to think about a better, quicker way of doing something. There is no rocket science or mystique involved – it is just that most of the time we are not consciously aware that we possess these natural thinking abilities. Thinking in these creative ways is as old as humankind itself, the following story is a way of bringing this fact home to children.

Honey, I'm home!

Think of cave people with rumbling bellies out hunting for their dinner. Initially, they used natural objects – branches of trees or stones – to hunt wild animals. Over time they came to notice that certain shapes of stones were more effective than others. They might have spent all their days looking for sharp-pointed stones until they thought: 'This is daft. What if I spend less time wandering around, and instead figure out a way to make the stones more pointed myself? Let's try it and see. What if I try bashing this stone against that stone? Brilliant, that helps me shape a stone into a point! Right, figured that bit out! But I can't make the whole stone too sharp all around the edges or I won't be able to hold it very well or throw it straight. I can't guarantee that the sharp bit is going to hit the target every time either. I need something to guide it. What if I used some of those branches we use to hunt with, and fix the stone on to the end of one? Brilliant, my idea works! I'm a genius! Can't wait to tell the kids when I get back to the cave ... Honey, I'm home!'

Thinking about a wobbly supermarket trolley that is driving you mad as we shop for your dinner today isn't of course any different. As soon as we start thinking like this we are switching our mindset to a higher level of thinking. Instead of accepting everything as just the way it is, we are opening our mind up to thinking about new possibilities and saying instead: '*What if?*'

Tinker, tailor, chef, physicist ...

Thinking critically about things to take our thinking to a higher level, and coming up with brilliant new ideas is for every sphere of human endeavour. We can all do it. The field or subject really doesn't matter. It is important for all children to grasp this point. The media can sometimes project stereotypical images into our children's minds that suggest that the only people capable of having new ideas are from a certain field – science for example. Whether a person is an entrepreneur, doctor, gardener or fashion designer, they are all capable of developing higher levels of thinking to unlock their creativity and come up with great ideas. Which subject children excel in isn't important, their ideas are. If your child has any doubts about this, then the following case study is a great one to share with them to help them see creativity is for everyone, and all walks of life.

Scrumptious creations!

It seems that as the Western world has less time to cook, it has also become fascinated with cookery! Worldwide we have seen a huge increase in the number of chefs on our TV screens. We get home from a busy day, collapse on the sofa and look at the mouth-watering recipes they create. And create is the important bit here. Each chef has their own special recipes that they thought up. How did they do it? Like the cave people who wanted a better way to hunt for their dinner, they asked themselves a simple question: 'What if?'

For example, a chef might wonder: 'What if I take the basic recipe for pancakes and add a few things of my own? What if I add a few different flavours and ingredients?' Then they go away, do some experimenting and, hey presto, they create a scrumptious new recipe for pancakes!

One famous and highly successful chef in Britain, Marco Pierre White (the youngest chef ever to be awarded the prestigious honour for cuisine of two Michelin stars), gives dates to some of the recipes he creates. Why not? They are *his* recipes! He was the one who thought them up and created them! The fact that all his dishes are quickly consumed makes them no less creative and exciting than writing a new piece of music, designing a fantastic new engine or anything else! Each of these ideas resulted from using a high level of thinking to unlock individual creativity.

Learning to fly

The activities in this chapter have been carefully structured to show children the power of their own creative thinking. Step by step, the activities use trigger words, phrases and questions that they will come to associate with unleashing their own higher levels of thinking and creativity. As with all the activities in this book, the emphasis is on learning through doing so that children learn all they need to know for themselves.

The first activity will enable your child to:

★   Use open-ended questions to ignite their imagination;
★   Tap into their higher-level thinking by letting their creative ability shine through.

Activity 7: The 'What if?' Game

In order to learn how to begin tapping into their own abilities, the first thing your child needs to do is practise letting free their creative thinking; the 'what if' game enables them to do this. In a relaxed yet focused way this activity enables them to experience their own ability to think creatively by asking the open-ended question: '*What if?*'

How to help children get the best out of this activity

Introduce the activity as the 'what if' game. Let your child choose which 'what if' question they would like to start with. Then suggest that they copy the question down on a piece of paper. Let them know they have two minutes to come up with as many ideas as they can, and to make a list of them as they go along. When the time is up and they have finished making the list, praise their ideas and ask them how they came up with each one.

For example, in answer to question a) below, they might have put 'the beach'. When you ask how they came up with the idea they might say something like: '*A beach might be a place a cat would want to drive to because there are fish in the sea. Cats like fish, so I thought 'beach!'* Then let them choose two other 'what if' questions and do the same thing. If they are feeling adventurous and energetic they can do all of them! If at any time they need a kick-start to get them thinking their own thoughts, show them the pictures below. Alternatively, looking at the pictures is an excellent way to round the activity off. By letting them see the 'what if' question associated with funny images that make them laugh, the whole activity becomes a more memorable one for children. It also serves to begin a positive cycle of thinking in their minds – creative thinking is a natural and fun mental activity!

WHAT IF?
a)   What if cats could drive? Where do you think they would drive to?
b)   What if dogs could cook? What 'goodies' do you think they would mix into their birthday cake?
c)   What if all the stripes fell off a tiger? Would it still be a tiger?
d)   What if the three little pigs and the big bad wolf had become great friends? Do you think they would all have been able to live happily ever after?
e)   What if flowers could talk? What sorts of things would they say?

What if ...?

What if dogs could cook?

What if cats could drive?

What if a tiger lost its stripes?

What if the 3 little pigs and wolf became great friends?

What if flowers could talk?

Activity 8: Fact or Fiction?

The last activity showed your child that by asking the simple, open-ended question, '*What if?*', they could kick-start their creative thinking and come up with a whole range of brilliant and imaginative ideas. Using our imagination is one way of thinking that leads us to having great ideas. Learning how to question what we already know about things and look for new possibilities is another. Children need to know both of these tricks of genius to maximize upon their own natural abilities. In this activity your child is going to learn how to use their powers of critical thinking and logic in formulating their own ideas and opinions.

Learning how to use our powers of critical thinking and logic to sort fact from fiction is an important trick of genius. It is only by continuing to question our knowledge – or lack of it – that we make advances and new discoveries. History has shown this time and again. We find it amusing today to think that at one time learned people were convinced that the Earth was flat, and were flabbergasted when they found out it was in fact round! To make this discovery, it was only by asking a 'what if' question that thinking about the shape of the Earth was taken to a higher level. Plus, daring to think *critically* about the old 'Flat Earth' theory produced logical reasons as to why this did not accurately describe the true state of the Earth. Great thinkers have always known how to use critical thinking to take them to a higher level of thinking – whatever the topic. Your child can learn how to do this for themselves too in the next activity.

How to help children get the best out of this activity

In each case below they are presented with a quandary. In each scenario they are prompted to come up with three reasons why something could, and three reasons why something could not be possible. They are being asked to think about whether something is fact or fiction. When they have thought about the quandary critically in this way, your child is then invited to give their own ideas and opinions about the topic. Each time your child does this they are learning how to:

★   Assess information for themselves;
★   Weigh up facts against fiction;
★   Think critically.

After they have done this activity, give them time to unpack their ideas, logic and reasoning in each case, using a free-flowing conversation with them to discuss what they came up with. Then explain to them that what they have just done is something smart people do all the time: they think clearly, using questions and reasons to come up with their own brilliant ideas. To round off, let your child see the quick summary of the thinking pattern they have used in the 'The Five Keys to Crystal Clear Thinking' on the following page.

The Five Keys to Crystal Clear Thinking

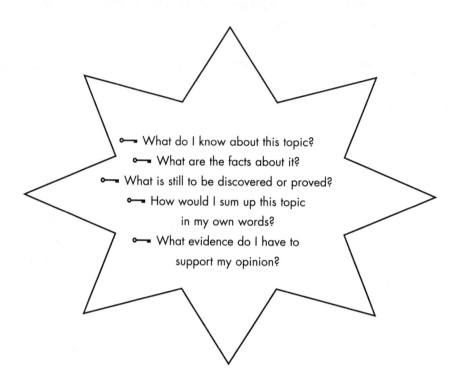

- What do I know about this topic?
- What are the facts about it?
- What is still to be discovered or proved?
- How would I sum up this topic in my own words?
- What evidence do I have to support my opinion?

(I) DRAGONS – ANCIENT MONSTERS OR FAIRY TALES?

3 reasons there may have been monsters like dragons:	3 reasons dragons are just fairy tales:

My thoughts on the subject:

(II) CARS – THE GREATEST INVENTION EVER?

3 reasons why cars could be the greatest invention ever:	3 reasons why cars might not be the greatest invention ever:

My thoughts on the subject:

(III) HOLIDAYS IN SPACE – COULD THEY EVER HAPPEN?

3 reasons why they could happen:	3 reasons why they might not happen:

My thoughts on the subject:

CHECKPOINT

Q: **How can my child benefit from this thinking skill in their school work?**

A: **Your child benefits on two levels. First, by learning how to think about information they encounter in a crystal clear way, your child will see that knowledge is not just something that is created by others and passed on to them. They can have a piece of the action themselves! What do I mean? Most of the time at school, children are busy 'cramming' facts, without ever letting themselves stand** back to think about what new areas still need to be discovered or explored in a topic. Their thinking becomes sluggish and they can unknowingly overlook the exciting fact that there is still much to be investigated and revealed in any topic. With the activities in this chapter your child is learning to ask questions that will keep their learning alive and exciting. They are learning to keep their thinking sharp and their mind alert to new ideas. Result: when your child is learning at school they will automatically begin to do two things at once, without 'thinking' about it:

★ Gather knowledge;
★ Think through topics for themselves.

Both of these are skills that education systems around the world are gradually beginning to recognize as key in preparing children for life and work in the 21st century. Knowing what these skills are and how to tap into them will put your child ahead of the game. First: they will know how to question things in classroom discussions, and how to develop their own informed opinions on topics – whether answering an examination question or doing their homework. Second: the sooner your child starts using critical thinking, the more skilful they will get at it, so that they easily become accustomed to doing this every day at school. Of equal importance, they will also have learned another trick of genius into the bargain!

Whenever your child has just learned a new topic at school and is being asked to write about it for homework, a project or in an examination, they can use the Five Keys to Crystal Clear Thinking to help them ensure that they produce a well-thought out, balanced and logical answer. This is sure to impress everyone!

At the same time, your child can practise using this clear thinking pattern to assess all the information that bombards them every day. For example, when they are watching television programmes or reading magazines with advertisements in them, they can get into the habit of using their own independent thinking about products they see instead of passively accepting all the 'blurb' that is blasted at them as undisputed fact!

From the activities they have just completed, they have become aware of two great natural abilities they possess: *imagination* and the ability to *think* critically. Next, your child will learn that by *combining* these two abilities they will be following a pattern of thinking that unlocks creativity – naturally.

Warning – apprentice genius at work!

"There is no use trying," said Alice. "One can't believe impossible things."

"I dare say you haven't had much practise" said the Hatter. "When I was your age, I always did it for half an hour a day. Why, sometimes I've believed as many as six impossible things before breakfast."

LEWIS CARROLL

Genius thinkers do all of the time what most of us have forgotten or were never taught to do – practise having ideas, and develop the self-confidence to believe in our ideas when we have them!

It is common sense when you think about it. How can we come up with any creative ideas if we do not have the opportunity to have a go at it regularly? And how can we have faith in our ideas if we never get the opportunity to discuss them and gain positive feedback from those around us?

No one has a monopoly on good ideas

No one has a monopoly on good ideas, so why shoot ourselves down whenever we get one? When any of us is critical about something and decides we could come up with a better idea ourselves, typically we laugh it off and talk ourselves out of it! Not convinced? Any of the following sound familiar?

◆   'It's probably too simple!'
◆   'Someone else has probably done it already!'
◆   'People probably wouldn't take it seriously!'
◆   'It probably would never work anyway …'

There are an awful lot of 'probablies' here aren't there? If any potential genius thought like this all the time they would never get anywhere. The truth is, whether we are thinking critically about the design of a supermarket trolley or that of a plane, we do not know whether our idea will work – *until we try it out.*

Do you think that Einstein, Mozart or da Vinci ever sat there, thought of a brilliant idea, and then stopped themselves short by saying: '*This will never work?*' On a bad day maybe, but most of the time their thinking hinged on another way of thinking: '*Why not?*' They got so busy thinking and experimenting with their ideas that they forgot everything else. Result: *maximum creativity!*

Children can learn how to think like this too. In the next activity they are going to combine their critical thinking skills with their imagination to come up with some ideas of their own, about a wide range of objects we use in the world around us.

Unlock creativity in two simple words – 'Why not?'

By asking themselves with two simple words: 'why not?', your child can learn for themselves their own power of creativity. Used correctly the following activity enables children to:

★   Value their creative ability;
★   Practise presenting their ideas to others;
★   Have confidence in their ideas.

What do I mean by 'used correctly'? Remember those black and white pictures of pioneering inventors donning wings in an attempt to fly? They looked hilarious, but then most good ideas do at some time or another in their development. As your child unleashes their creative thinking in the following activity they are going to make some suggestions and ideas that may cause you to want to laugh. When I have done this activity with children, they have come up with planes that run off chocolate bars, dynamite and fireworks (wonderfully exciting but messy!) or are environmentally friendly by being pedal powered (great for passengers on long-haul flights eh?!).

By all means laugh *with* them at their suggestions, but not *at* them, no matter how tempting it might be! Otherwise we are back to our wobbly supermarket trolley and having no confidence in our ideas for improving it. That would be teaching your child how *not* to think like a genius. So, at this stage, remember to focus on what is really important: no matter how bizarre or fantastical their ideas and suggestions are, go with them and praise *them all* lovingly! Age is not an issue here either. It does not matter whether your child is in junior or high school – the same thing applies.

Sparking off an upward spiral of creativity

Praising your child's ideas is not just an exercise in confidence building. The whole activity here acts like a kind of 'Trojan horse' to set up a positive thinking cycle deep within their mind.

- By rewarding their ideas with praise, their psyche builds a positive association between using patterns of creative thinking and a fun experience.
- This in turn sparks off an upward spiral of creativity in your child's mind.
- Once their mind learns that thinking creatively pays off, it will be happy to do this again and again.
- Result: your child will be confident in, and enjoy using their creative ability not just in school, but throughout life.

Activity 9: Why not?

How to help children get the best out of this activity

If you are introducing this activity straight after activities 7 and 8, then children will be in top gear to think creatively as their minds will already be in 'creativity mode'. If it has been a couple of days or weeks (or months!) since they last did it, then before moving on, it is a good idea to get your child's thinking back into 'creativity mode'. Zipping back through the 'What if?' activity again they will be charged up and ready to go.

As soon as you are both ready, introduce the activity below as a game called 'Why not?' Tell them that the only rule of the game is that they are to let their ideas and imagination go wild! Ask them to choose any *one* of the challenges and, as they go through the activity, jot their ideas down on a piece of paper. If they like, they can use drawings instead of notes to demonstrate their ideas.

For each challenge there is a time limit. Keep to it! By putting a time element into the activity, the idea is that children will have less time to be concerned with how their idea sounds. Instead, they will be focusing upon thinking up as many ideas as they can.

As soon as they have completed one of the challenges, go through their ideas with them. Remember that the precise nature of their ideas is not important here – *developing confidence in freely expressing their creativity is.* They don't have to stop at just the one challenge –they can do as many as they like. The choice is theirs.

1. YOU HAVE 5 MINUTES TO DESIGN A BETTER LUNCH BOX FOR SCHOOL.

a)   Think about **three** things you love and three things you hate about lunch boxes!

b)   Now, **let your ideas and imagination run wild!** Design a new kind of lunch box that *you* would like? Why not!? Your ideas are as good as anyone else's!? Think:

o   What colour and shape would it be?
o   What special features would it have?
o   Why would everyone want one?

Get your thinking cap on! Go! Go! Go!

2. YOU HAVE 5 MINUTES TO DESIGN A BETTER PLANE FOR THE 21ST CENTURY.

a)   Think about **three** things you love and three things you hate about planes today!

b)   Now, **let your ideas and imagination run wild!** Design a plane that *you* would like to fly in? Why not!? Your ideas are as good as anyone else's! Think:

- What would the new plane look like?
- What would the seats be like?
- What kind of fuel would it run off?

Get your thinking cap on! Go! Go! Go!

3. YOU HAVE 5 MINUTES TO DESIGN A BETTER HOME COMPUTER.

a)   Think about **three** things you love and three things you hate about computers!

b)   Now, **let your ideas and imagination run wild!** Design a new kind of computer that *you* would like. Why not!? Your ideas are as good as anyone else's! Think:

- What colour (or colours) will it be?
- What shape will it be?
- Will it just sit on your desk or will it be able to move around?

Get your thinking cap on! Go! Go! Go!

Reinventing the wheel

As they did the last activity, your child has been reinventing the wheel. How? They have been working through a pattern of thinking that has lead to innovation, invention and 'genius' discoveries – for centuries. OK, so they may not have gone the full hog and actually invented a new plane or whatever (then again, they may have – why not!?), but they have begun to experience the pattern of thinking involved in creating something new – whether it is a new washing machine or a new toy. You realize this, but they need to *learn* this empowering fact for themselves. Activity 10 is designed to do just that. By looking at stories of how good inventions happened, your child will discover that:

- ◆ Every good idea started in someone's head;
- ◆ In history good ideas have always occurred to all kinds of people;
- ◆ Getting an idea from vision to reality follows a creative *pattern*;
- ◆ By trying out new ideas combined with a determination to succeed, inventions and discoveries are made.

Activity 10: I've Got an Idea!

Each of the case studies in this activity summarizes how the birth of an idea can lead to a new discovery or invention. Choose who will start first, then read through the case studies together with your child. After you have done this there is a 'conversation starter' question which provides children with the opportunity to pick out and discuss with you the pattern that unites all these diverse people and inventions together: the pattern of creativity.

From cocoa bean to melt in your mouth!

As you bite into a milk chocolate bar, have you ever wondered how chocolate was invented? The word chocolate comes from an old Spanish word which was borrowed from the ancient Aztec civilization in South America! (The word is *xocolatl* – meaning 'bitter water'.) The key ingredient of chocolate, cocoa, comes from the cocoa bean which was grown by the Aztecs. In the 16th century, Spanish sailors became regular visitors to the shores of South America and eventually came to conquer the Aztecs. The Spanish saw that the Aztecs drank a 'bitter water' made from cocoa beans and they took this idea with them back to Europe. The idea of the cocoa bean drink caught on in Europe, mainly amongst the very rich.

How then did we get chocolate bars from all of this? The cocoa bean has a fat in it which melts at, or slightly below normal body temperature: this is cocoa butter. This is one of the ingredients that makes chocolate so attractive to us because it melts in the mouth. In the early 19th century, Conrad Van Houten successfully experimented with an idea he had to make a press that could separate the cocoa butter from the cocoa bean.

A way was then needed to bring together the melting sensation of cocoa butter, the sweetness of sugar and the flavour of the cocoa bean. If this could be done then a kind of chocolate would have been invented. But it was easier said than done. Getting all these ingredients to work together to produce something good to eat was a difficult one. It took time, patience and persistence to perfect.

It is not known for certain who actually invented the first eating chocolate, but in the mid-19th century the English company Fry and Sons put the first eating chocolate on sale in Britain. However, this was still not a *milk* chocolate and was based mainly on cocoa butter.

So how did milk come to be added into the mixture for chocolate? At the end of the 19th century, a Swiss man named Daniel Peters experimented with the idea of adding different milk products to liquid chocolate. He kept researching how milk could be used with chocolate. He kept adjusting the ingredients in his mixture, until he eventually made a breakthrough. He found that if liquid chocolate was mixed with sugar and condensed milk, and then mixed with cocoa butter, a *milk chocolate* could be made. Mixing all these ingredients together to get it just right takes time and skill, and it is greatly simplified here. But all the patience and time paid off and it worked! Peters then worked together with Henri Nestlé and together they are recorded as having produced the first milk chocolate bar. By the end of the 19th century, milk chocolate finally became widely available for everyone to buy.

So next time you are about to sink your teeth into a milk chocolate bar, remember, it took a lot of thinking, time, energy and experimenting to create it! No wonder it tastes so good!

A brilliant new hair product!

Madam C.J. Walker was a self-made millionaire and one of the most successful businesswomen and entrepreneurs in America in the 19th and 20th centuries. Her life and inventions are a story of determination and self-belief. Madam C.J. Walker was born as Sarah Breedlove, the daughter of two former African-American slaves who lived and worked in Louisiana. Both her parents died when Sarah was a little girl. Sarah was to become Sarah Breedlove Walker when she married. She and her husband had a daughter, but not long afterwards her husband died and Sarah had to struggle to support herself and her little girl alone. She achieved this by getting a job working as a washerwoman in St Louis, Missouri.

While working full time, and looking after her daughter, she came up with a brilliant idea – a hair lotion that would soften women's hair, making wavy hair become easier to straighten with combs. Before Sarah had this idea, women had just used hot combs and irons to straighten out the kinks in their hair. By carefully experimenting, researching and reviewing the ingredients of her special formula, Sarah adjusted her formula until she got exactly the result she wanted. She had invented a revolutionary new hair product.

Sarah persisted with her idea and marketed it. She became known as Madam C.J. Walker. The hair treatment she invented became known as the 'Walker System', used by women throughout the world. Madam C.J. Walker set up an extremely successful cosmetics company. She was a great lady, inventor, businesswoman and became a benefactor for charities.

The first boy to fly

Today we take planes and helicopters for granted. But it took the time, energy and determination of many inventors to bring us to where we are today. Sir George Cayley (1773–1857) was one such person. He was a scientist who dedicated his life to discovering how to build a craft that people could fly in. One of the first ideas he had was to observe how birds flew. He noted that when in flight the bird's wings were arched.

Cayley then started to experiment with different designs for a flying craft. He began by experimenting with glider designs. At first these were not successful. He didn't give up. He kept on experimenting, researching and adjusting his different designs, using kites as prototypes. Eventually, he was successful, making a glider able to carry a person.

One of the first persons alleged to have actually experienced flight in one of Cayley's experimental gliders was not an adult but a boy! The name of the boy is not known, but he is recorded as successfully flying in one of Cayley's gliders for a short time in the mid-19th century.

Through his pioneering efforts into the science of flight, Cayley was able to discover much about the basic but essential scientific rules that enable aircraft to fly. Sir George Cayley's early work contributed to the work of other inventors to bring us to the aircraft with which we are all familiar today.

Question for discussion

 Q: What was it about all of these people that made them successful in their inventions?

A: All of these people were different. But they all had ideas, and they all followed a *pattern* to achieve their invention – what was it? To help enrich this discussion with your child read on.

Patterns of creativity

Each of the people here, who were involved in making a breakthrough, discovery or invention, went through a pattern of thinking that lead to success. It is a pattern of thinking that leads to outstanding creativity in any field – as each of the diverse topics covered in the case studies demonstrates. What was the pattern that all of these people followed to create their discoveries? The following acronyms will help children remember. Each of the people involved:

> Created a new idea;
> Researched how they could make it happen;
> Experimented with different ways of achieving it;
> Adjusted their thinking when and where they had to;
> Tried their ideas out;
> Ended up with the result they wanted!

At the same time they also had:

> Belief in themselves;
> Energy to overcome obstacles;
> Learned the importance of persistence;
> Invested time in their ideas;
> Enthusiasm for what they were doing;
> Faith in their ideas.

Now that your child has completed the activity, let them write the acronyms down on a large piece of paper and pin it on their bedroom wall or if they have one their notice board. By having these acronyms close to hand your child will never forget the power of the creative ability they possess, and to have belief in *themselves* – always! By thinking about these case studies your child will see that when a person brings together their creativity and

The Wheel of Creativity

absolute belief in their own ability, they can make fantastic discoveries that change the way we live – whether it is in hairdressing, confectionery or aviation.

Activity II: The Wheel of Creativity

There is nothing new about this pattern of thinking – it is older than the wheel! Explain this fact to children by showing them the Wheel of Creativity on page 129. As they follow the wheel around, they will see how all good ideas, including their own, *can* come to fruition by following a tried and tested pattern of creative thinking, learning and doing. But don't blame me if in a few weeks' time your child has secretly built a new kind of space craft in their bedroom! Before they decide to do that, there is just one last activity and a major contract for your child to sign. A promise to remember how brilliant they are!

Contract to Celebrate Brilliant Me!

Name: Age:

I hereby declare that I always have faith in my abilites, ideas and creativity because:

1. I am brilliant (and modest too!)
2. I have absolute faith in me!
3. I have absolute belief in my abilites!
4. I enjoy using my gifts and talents!
5. I use clear thinking to think things through for myself!
6. I value the ideas I get when I think creatively!
7. I never let anyone put my ideas down!
8. I am always as good as the next person!
9. Why do I know all of this?
10. Because I know how to think like a genius!

Signed:

Date:

Witnessed by:

Brainbox

① Thinking creatively is something we can all do naturally.

① Having faith in our ideas doesn't always come naturally.

① The trick of genius is to believe in our ideas.

① We can teach our children how to tap into their ability to think critically and creatively and believe in their ideas.

① After doing the activities in this chapter your child will have learned how to unlock their creativity, and to have faith in their ideas – always.

① A creative thinking pattern occurs when new inventions and discoveries are made.

① A person thinks up an idea, experiments to try it out, thinks about it critically and keeps adjusting it until they come up with exactly what they want.

① This is not a new pattern of thinking. It is the wheel of mental creativity that invented the wheel!

After your child has done the activities in this chapter, be warned! The 'time for bed' negotiation routine may reach a higher level of thinking when your child decides to apply their newly fine-tuned thinking skills to reach the conclusion that *they* are not ready for bed. If they do this, you know what to do, don't you? Challenge them to put their newly learned creative thinking skills to work to invent a new world-beating device that switches children off at bedtime! That should keep them quiet for months and if they succeed it will make you all a fortune.

"I've just got one more thing to do and I'll be right there."

Masters of their subject

What do Mozart, Einstein, da Vinci, Charles Babbage (the inventor of the precursor to the modern-day computer), Marie Curie (the scientist who discovered radium), or the chef Marco Pierre White all have in common? Creativity, certainly, and also mastery of their subject; somewhere in their life they each took charge of their learning so that they could make the best use of their gifts in each of their own individual fields. Section IV shows your child how to do this for themselves, starting with their magic mind, and how we learn naturally.

section four

How to Learn Like a Genius

Chapter 7

Our Magic Minds

The best gift ever

It is crazy when you think about it. As soon as a child starts toddling around the house they become aware of, and dazzled by the 'magic' of the technology they find around them: televisions, computers, washing machines, mobile phones, dishwashers, battery-operated toys, fairy lights, digital music centres and so on. Then, much later at school, *if* your child is lucky, they might have a couple of classes about the most brilliant and superior 'technology' around – our brains. But the fact is, in the prime of their school years, our children can end up knowing more about how to get the best out of their mobile phone than how to get the best out of their own brain!

You and I know that the best gift your child will ever get is their brain. The first step in helping them to take charge of their own learning is to let them get inside their brain and find out how brilliant it is, and how they learn with it. No child should have to wait to know about this. It is essential knowledge for any budding geniuses out there, whether your child has their heart set on a career in soccer, acting, astrophysics, languages, computers or creative writing, they should be able to know the magic of their own mind. After all it's better than any pair of designer trainers. It's absolutely their own, and it will never go out of fashion.

Understanding the technology

Through no fault of our own, most of us went through our school years knowing no more than a couple of things about the human brain – it has got a lot of grey matter, we all have one, and 'undressed' it looks rather ugly! But if we had known in school how our brains work we might have saved ourselves a whole lot of unnecessary work and worry when it came to examinations and learning in general. With the information in this chapter, your child need not go through the same blind cycle. We can change all that and put them in the light about their brain with a few quick learning activities - today.

More brilliant than a galaxy of stars

In this chapter, together we are going to switch the focus of your child's attention from thinking about what they do with the *outside* of their head – top it with their treasured designer baseball cap, stick glitter on it, bounce a ball off it, colour it with purple-streaked hair, glue it with hair gel – to what goes on *inside* their head!

The easy-to-use activities in this chapter will help children not to think of their mind as a 'grey mass' so much as being something so dazzling, it is more brilliant than a galaxy of stars, and 'cooler' than the latest pop sensation! But before we move on, you might have a few burning questions of your own about our brains that you would like answering right here, right now.

FAQs

 Q: When does most of the brain growth happen in a child?

 A: When a child has reached their sixth year, the brain has usually grown to around 90% of maximum adult size.

 **Q:** People are either right-sided or left-sided thinkers aren't they?

 **A:** If I had a cheque for every time this question came up in sem-
inars I'd be retired by now! The separation of our abilities into
either left or right-brain thinking is an idea that has steadily
spread around the globe, like a rampant ivy plant! In the
process, it has left a lot of people feeling confused and even
demoralized about their abilities. Let's start by reminding ourselves of a few facts. Every day, all of us, whatever we are
doing, need to use *both* sides of our brains to operate successfully. Contrary to what anyone might tell you, none of us are like
dolphins with the potential to switch alternating sides of their
brain off. (If you feel that you, or someone you know, is an
exception to this rule, please contact your local marine biology
centre now!) In fact, the only people who are in the challenging
position of having to function with impaired connectivity
between their left and right brain, are those who have sustained
a stroke or other serious brain injury.

Never mind, left and right brain – think connectivity!

So where does the idea come from that we should somehow declare ourselves either left or right minded? Back in the 20th century, research into
brain function made a massive breakthrough. It was discovered that the left
and right hemispheres of the brain were linked to different kinds of mental activity. Mathematics, logic and language became linked with the left
hemisphere. Music, visual imagery and patterns became linked with the
right hemisphere. But – and this is a big but – crucial to the brain's normal
functioning, is the *connectivity* between the left and right hemispheres of
the brain. Connecting them is a structure called the corpus callosum. This
is built up of millions of nerve fibres and acts like a superhighway, carrying

information between the left and right hemispheres of the brain.

To illustrate what all this research tells us about how our brains work in practice, let's take the example of Mozart. Picture him working busily away in the 18th century composing his opera, *The Magic Flute*. If we tried to label Mozart as purely a right-minded thinker, it would not be an accurate description of the *actual* brain power he was using as he composed the opera. In practice he was using *both* sides of his brain to achieve this great work. The right hemisphere produced the musical tunes and rhythms, the left hemisphere produced the words and sequence of the opera. Mozart would have been a bit stuck therefore had both his left and right brain not been working together as they normally do!

Exceptional performance uses both sides of the brain

In the 21st century, research by neuroscientists has suggested that exceptional thinkers and learners are those who are able to maximize on this natural connectivity between the left and right sides of their brain. The neuroscientist Norbert Jausovec carried out an experiment to see what it was that made some children exceptionally good at mathematical problem-solving. He found that children who were able to process the problems fastest were engaging different parts of their brain, from both the left and right hemispheres, altogether.

But what happens if your child is good at lots of different things, for example mathematics (left brain) and creative arts (right brain). How does left–right brain theory explain *their* gifts? In response, this is another problem with trying to separate out people into left or right brained thinkers. The following case study illustrates this point vividly.

Da Vinci – left or right?

We can look at the achievements of the world-famous inventor, engineer and artist, Leonardo da Vinci in a number of different ways, but none of them would make any sense unless we thought about him using *both* sides of his brain together effectively.

Da Vinci was a highly accomplished artist (right brain), but he was an equally accomplished scientist (left brain). As we know, he managed to combine all of his talents in his work and career, and this was a brilliant achievement, but it should not be seen as in any way impossible today. What do I mean? As far as we know, no one in da Vinci's time was busy trying to force his broad spectrum of talents into the narrow definition of either a right- or left-brained thinker! The world might have been robbed of his genius if someone had tried to do this, and poor da Vinci had been made to choose between a career in *either* science *or* art.

The point is, no one should have to make this choice. Indeed, some of the most exciting careers available to our children in the 21st century are those which occur at the crossroads between diverse disciplines. Computer graphics, for instance, is a fabulously creative field that stands at the crossroads of scientific and artistic ability. A person needs to develop a diverse range of abilities to succeed. Imagine what Leonardo da Vinci could have achieved had he been around today and working in computer graphics!

For all the reasons discussed here, slapping a label on someone as either a right- or left-brained thinker/learner can be sloppy, and misrepresentative of a person's individual abilities. So do not let anyone try to pigeon-hole your child's abilities so easily. The reality is that children are considerably more complicated than that. Indeed we all are!

FAQ

 Q: Are men and women's brains the same size?

 A: They are not the same weight but, in this instance, size does not matter. Given a problem-solving situation, women and men figure things out at the same speed, but they tend to use different parts of the brain in different ways to reach the same solution. Typically, women have a greater brain to bodyweight ratio than men, because men tend to be physically larger than women. On average a female brain weighs 1.25 kg and a male brain 1.35 kg. The idea that brain weight or size, or even the shape of our heads, has anything to do with mental ability belongs to the Victorian era. So, if you don't want to appear about three centuries out of date with your thinking, don't mention brain sizes!

Hearts and minds

In learning, pain doesn't equal gain. While there is no substitute for investing time and energy in learning, there are more effective and much more enjoyable ways of learning than by simply slogging away at something in the hope of remembering it! Although we can learn from bad experiences and making mistakes, when we learn a lesson through a traumatic experience, our minds are likely to attempt to delete the memory and send it to the 'recycle bin'. The memory will be retained in our minds somewhere, but retrieving it might be so painful that we would rather leave it where it is. On the other hand, when we are in a relaxed and happy state we can learn without even thinking about it. If they are to know how to tap into this natural ability to learn effectively, your child must first be able to understand how our minds work, and the importance of feeling good when they are learning.

Emotion and learning – if you are happy and you know it ... you learn!

Why does emotion play such an important part in our learning? Some of the ways our brains work emulate the way a computer might work. For example, the logical sequencing involved in lifting a glass of water from the table and bringing it to our lips could be achieved using a computer-operated mechanical arm. Similarly, many of us have played a computer at chess or cards. The logic of these games is primarily linear and follows repeated rules. Again, as with the logical sequencing involved in lifting a glass of water, the action is more or less mechanical. We might get passionate about losing a game of chess, but the computer doesn't fall over laughing with victory! Sometimes, the idea of being able to sever our logic from our emotions is a tempting one. But love it or hate it (there goes emotional thought again!) none of us are purely rational creatures. Our thought processes are inextricably linked with our emotions. So what are the implications of this for our child's learning?

Current research in the fields of education, child development and psychology indicates that far from being a mechanical 'input-output' exercise, learning involves both reason and emotion. Nestled in the 'heart of our brains' is the limbic system. Whenever we receive new information or think about things, the limbic system acts as a conduit, transferring instinctual impulses into rational thoughts. The limbic system is like a huge processing unit with the task of reconciling our emotions with rational thought in our minds.

The limbic system therefore has a crucial role to play in our learning. When we are feeling happy about our learning we make a better job of it. Your child will learn this for themselves later in this section, but first they can learn the information that has been summarized here for you for *themselves*. If you chose to begin the activities in this book with those in this Section you will note that they are all in a question and answer format. This is because they are grounded in *learning by discovery*, rather than 'information download'. The reasons for this were given in Section III in full, but for your convenience, they are summarized again for you here:

♦   Learning by questioning and reasoning for themselves, enables your child to become a better thinker and learner – all at the same time;
♦   Praising and rewarding your child to think and learn in this way helps their mind to link learning with an enjoyable and exciting activity;
♦   This creates an upward spiral of thinking and learning in which your child is continually developing confidence in their own ideas, thoughts and abilities.

Activity 12: 'Meet Your Magic Mind'

At the end of this activity your child will have learned that:

♦   Their mind is fantastic;
♦   The brain's capacity for learning is *limitless*;
♦   Male and female brains are equal;
♦   Energy within the brain is *awesome*;
♦   Their mind is better than magic – it has *real* power!

How to help children get the best out of this activity

In this activity they are shown a series of facts about their 'magic minds'. These facts appear in the stars on the illustrations on pages 145 and 146. The objective is to let them explore the facts about the brain for *themselves*.

They can choose which set of questions they want to start with first. The purpose of this is to enable them to see the benefits of taking charge of their own learning – *they* get to find out what they want first. Having control of our learning makes us all more motivated. Rather than being a passenger in our learning, we are sat firmly in the driving seat – so we are able to decide which route we are going to take to reach our next destination.

Introduce the activity to your child by its title. Inform them that they can start with any set of questions they like, and that all the information they need is in the illustrations. After they have finished, you can go through the answers with them, discussing each topic as you go along.

Fabulous facts about my magic mind – part I

Q: What travels as fast as a sports car?
A: ....

Q: What are neurons? What do they look like (draw one if you like)?
A: ....

Q: What number connects our brain cells with the stars in space?
A: ....

Q: How much of our oxygen is used up by our brains?
A: ....

Q: What has the power to light up a light bulb every minute?
A: ....

Fabulous Facts about my Magic Mind Part I

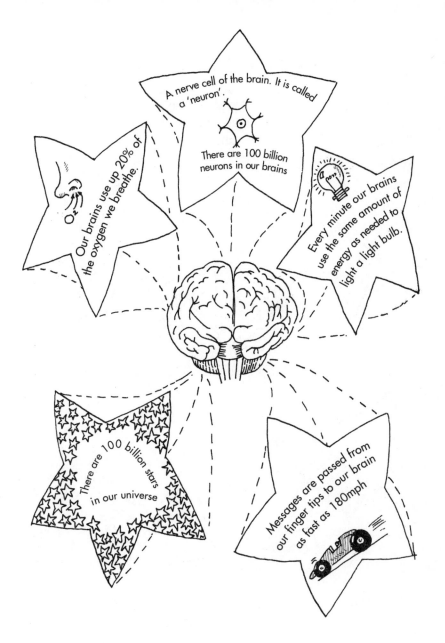

A nerve cell of the brain. It is called a 'neuron'.

There are 100 billion neurons in our brains

Our brains use up 20% of the oxygen we breathe.

Every minute our brains use the same amount of energy as needed to light a light bulb.

There are 100 billion stars in our universe

Messages are passed from our finger tips to our brain as fast as 180mph

Fabulous Facts about my Magic Mind Part II

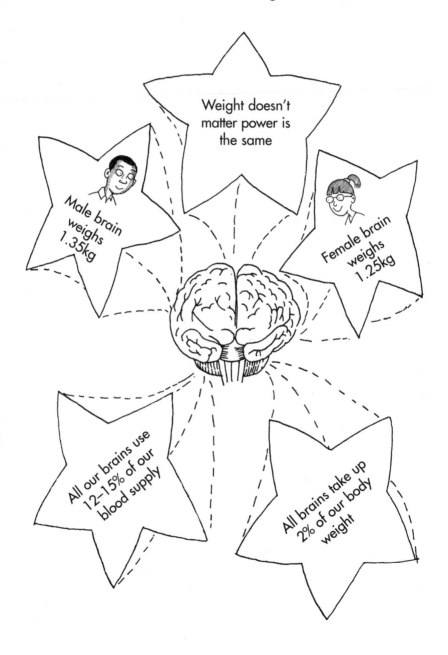

Fabulous facts about my magic mind – part II

Q: What is the weight of a female brain?
A: ....

Q: What is the weight of a male brain?
A: ....

Q: Is brain weight important?
A: ....

Q: Our brains are a super-lightweight and mobile 'computer': What percentage of our bodyweight do our brains take up?
A: ....

Q: Our brains burn up a lot of energy. How much of our blood supply does our brain take up?
A: ....

OK! So now your child has learned the basics about their 'Magic Mind'. Now they need to know how the major bits of 'hardware' are put together! This next activity ensures that your child knows as much about how their own brain works as they do about any home computer or mobile phone.

Activity 13: Left + Right Makes Me Bright!

By the end of this activity your child will know that:

◆   The left side of their brain deals with mathematics, sequence and language;
◆   The right side of their brain deals with music, rhythm and pictures;

My Left and My Right Makes me Bright!

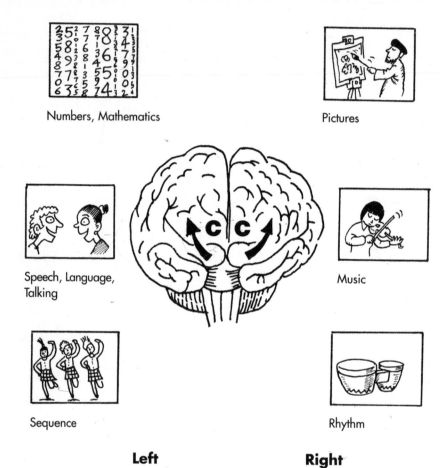

Numbers, Mathematics

Pictures

Speech, Language, Talking

Music

Sequence

Rhythm

Left   **Right**

★ **C**orpus **C**allosum is a thick band of nerve fibres.
★ The **CC** is a super highway. It connects the left and right sides of the brain.
★ Using left and right together is what Mozart did and what popstars do when they write songs!

- Their brain uses both sides of their brain together every day;
- A superhighway of nerve fibres connects the left and the right brain;
- Being able to use both sides of the brain *together* is what makes them so bright;
- Mozart composed operas by using his left *and* right brain;
- Pop musicians today write a hit song by using their left *and* right brain.

CHECKPOINT

Q: **What happens when someone is left-handed rather than right-handed?**

A: **The functions associated with the left and right hemispheres of the brain may be reversed when this is the case. If your child is left-handed then you can point this out, whilst also informing them that:**

- **This is perfectly OK;**
- **Not all geniuses are right-handed;**
- **It would be a pretty boring world if we were all the same!**

Remember: the most important point of this activity is not which side of the brain does what, or whether we are right- or left-handed. The message is that what is truly magical about our minds is that they bring so much power together inside our heads!

How to help children get the best out of this activity

To start, let them explore the information in the illustration on page 148. Then, if you like, discuss the information before they begin the activity, using the further examples below to enable your child to get a full grasp of the different terms used. By using the pictures and the examples below, they have a great opportunity to explore this topic for themselves, before doing the pencil activity further on.

Left Brain

SEQUENCE
Step by step – doing logical or mechanical kinds of things. For example:

♦   Climbing stairs step by step;
♦   Putting something in order: A, B, C, or 1, 2, 3.

MATHEMATICAL
Using numbers to make links between things. For example:

♦ $1 + 4 = 5$;
♦ $4x + 2 = 14$.

LANGUAGE
Using language to express yourself. For example:

♦   Talking and writing;
♦   Enjoying the *words* of a song.

Right Brain

PICTURES AND IMAGES
Describing our world, and seeing things using pictures, rather than using words. For example:

- Painting;
- Our houses or cities, seeing the world in '3D'.

RHYTHM
Something we feel, hear and can move to. For example:

- Feeling the rhythm in a song;
- Following the rhythm in poetry.

'Higher and higher flies the kite,
Bouncing and bobbing, out of sight'

MUSICAL
Listening and focusing upon sounds, rather than words. For example:

- Feeling happy or sad when we hear an instrument played;
- Enjoying the tune of a song.

It is a good idea to talk about the comparison between Mozart and modern-day singer/song writers. It is shown by the illustration above that to write a song involves both sides of their brain working together. By giving your child a context of how left/right brain thinking works together *in practice*, they are more likely to remember what they have learned throughout the whole activity.

Pencil Activity

Using the information on page 148, ask them to use a pencil (or coloured pencils) to connect the different kinds of activity with the different 'sides' of the brain. Tell them not to worry about letting their lines go through the 'CC', as this is exactly how the brain works; communicating information from the left to the right and vice versa, through the nerve fibres in the corpus callosum.

Left   **Right**

'CC'
(corpus callosum)
the superhighway of nerves
linking left and right brain activity

Music   Language   Mathematics

Pictures   Rhythm   Sequence

Q: What do the composer Mozart and pop artists who write songs have in common?

A: ....

Q: What does CC stand for?
A: C_ _ _ _ s C_ _ _ _ _ m

Q: What is the CC?
A: ....

Now that your child has learnt about the 'hardware', they can find out about the 'software' – how we actually think and learn. They need to understand (if they didn't already!) that what makes us so much more creative and magical than any home computer is that we mix rational thinking with our emotions and feelings, and that for this reason we learn best when we are happy. In short, they need to know the Magic Formula for Smart Learning. The following two activities enable your child to do just that.

Activity 14: My Magic Mind v. My Home Computer!

In this activity children can see how their brains work when they think and learn. Your child will come to know for themselves that:

♦   At the heart of our brain is the limbic system;
♦   The limbic system enables us to learn by using:

★ Emotion;
★ Thinking;
★ Knowledge.

♦   Spin-offs from our brain combining thinking, emotion and knowledge are that we are able to do many things that make our performance magical compared to a 'home computer'. These include:

★ Imagination;
★ Creativity;
★ Individual thoughts and ideas.

How to help children get the best out of this activity

Let them browse quickly through the illustration on page 154. Then let them know that they have just two minutes to discover all the answers to the questions below. Combining a challenge with a time limit increases motivation to learn and stops them worrying about new or different words, and getting on instead with the exciting bit – discovering new knowledge about their brain for themselves!

Six Brilliant Things my Magic Mind Has that a Computer Doesn't!

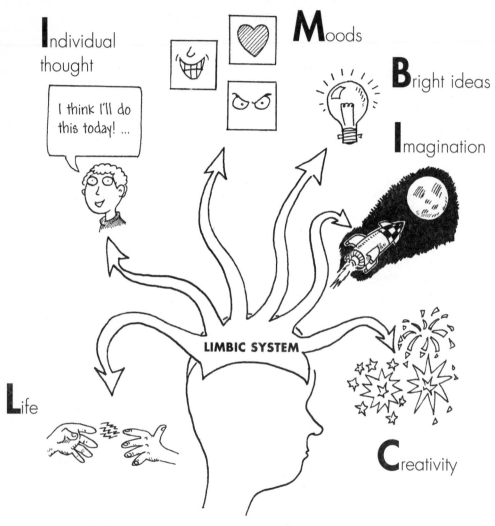

- ♦ The limbic system is in the centre of our brain.
- ♦ The limbic system is the 'heart' of our brain.
- ♦ It brings our thoughts, feelings and knowledge together.
- ♦ Being able to do this is what makes us so much cleverer than a computer!

Complete the six brilliant things that your Magic Mind has, but your home computer does not!

- ◆   L ....!
- ◆   Individual Thought!
- ◆   M ....!
- ◆   Bright Ideas!
- ◆   I ....!
- ◆   C ....!

Q: Together these initial letters spell 'LIMBIC' – where is this part of our brain?

A: ....

Q: The limbic system is clever. What three things does it bring together in our brains?

1   T...................
2   F...................
3   K ....

We think your child is a genius ...!

At the beginning of this chapter, I mentioned that your child would go away knowing that their brain was anything but grey, but that does not mean that their teacher's hair will not be instantly, (particularly if your child is still in junior school), when your child casually informs them that we have a corpus callosum and a limbic system ... Don't be surprised if you get a phone call from school telling you your child is a genius!

Guess what, Miss!

Activity 15: The Magic Formula for Smart Learning

Once your child has completed this activity, they will have in their mind a formula that they can apply for their own personal success in learning. The formula on page 158 purposely uses both pictures and words to make it easier and more fun for children to remember.

How to help children get the best out of this activity

Used in conjunction with all that they have learned in this chapter, this activity forms an excellent foundation for children to begin to personalize their own learning in chapter 9. If it has been some time since your child did the earlier activities in this chapter, refresh their minds first about their key points before diving straight into the Magic Formula for Smart Learning. That way, your child will be sure to have the maximum benefit from this short but effective activity. Let them spend a minute looking at the Magic Formula for Smart Learning. Cover up the formula and, using the symbols or words, let them write it out below for themselves, and answer the question below.

$$\ldots\ldots\ldots + \ldots\ldots\ldots = \ldots\ldots\ldots!$$

Q: Why is how we feel important when we are learning?

A: ....

The Magic Formula for Smart Learning

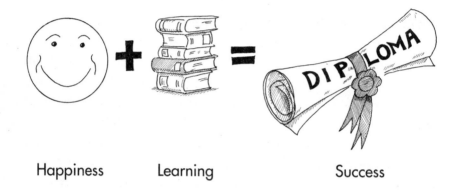

Happiness   Learning   Success

- Because our brains use feelings when we learn, how we feel when we are learning is very important.
- When we are happy we learn better.

In this chapter your child learned how their brain is put together and which parts are especially important in their learning. In the next chapter they will learn basic brain maintenance – how to run their brain better and keep it in tip-top condition. Fully equipped with this knowledge, and with what they learned in Section II, your child will be ready to learn like a genius. Your child will be ready to thumb print their learning to bring out their own unique and natural gifts and master learning for life.

Brainbox

- Children care no more about their mobiles than they do about their own brain.
- To harness and develop their abilities, they need to know how the brain works.
- Once a child understands how the brain works for themselves, they can use that knowledge to help them in their own learning.
- Although our brain is organized into left and right hemispheres it is connected by a superhighway that relays information back and forth.
- In a recent study to determine what made some children exceptionally good at problem-solving it was found that they maximized on using both their left *and* right brain hemispheres. Making best use of the connectivity between left and right we maximize upon our learning.
- The notion that we are either left- or right-brained thinkers falls apart when you take someone like Leonardo da Vinci. He need not be the exception, he could be the rule.
- The limbic system in the brain reconciles emotion with rational thought.
- If we are happy when we are learning, then we learn more effectively.

Chapter 8

Thinking Food

In a world dominated by adverts about faces and bodies on the TV, satellite, cable, internet and magazines, thinking about how what we eat, see and hear affects our brains, may not be the first thing that springs to mind! Keeping our brains in tip-top condition means taking all of this into consideration; what we input in terms of sights and sounds, as well as food, can affect our output. By the end of this chapter children will be qualified in brain maintenance, they will understand:

♦ How to switch the brain from 'screen saver mode' to ready and alert;
♦ The importance of fats in their diet for brain power;
♦ Exercise is good for their brain as well as the body;
♦ Certain kinds of music can help their minds think.

Finding the 'on' button for your brain

Ask any child how they switch on a computer, and even if we can't find the 'on' button *they* always can! As soon as a computer is switched on, the screen soon lights up and is ready to go (well most of the time!). By comparison, sometimes while our brains are technically 'on' we are not exactly ready to go. Of course, this could be because we are about to fall asleep or we are not very well – (or that we had one too many glasses of wine!).

But what about when we are in the middle of a meeting and sheer boredom is sending us to sleep? Is there anything we can do to 'jump start' our brains, apart from hogging the coffee machine, suggesting we turn the meeting into a karaoke contest or resigning!? Yes! We can 'brain-wash' ourselves. No, don't worry. I'm not suggesting that if you are falling asleep at work that you repeat the mantra: 'I get paid for this I can't fall asleep'. There is a better, much more effective way to get the best out of our brains: by taking charge of its physiology. Understanding how to take care of their brain is another step toward children taking charge of their learning. They can find out how to hit their brain's on button when required.

Both you and your child can do the following exercise whenever you find yourselves bored out of your skull but knowing you want to be alert. It provides an overall refresher for your mind and body and leaves you feeling revitalized mentally and physically— and it's so easy to do. No, it doesn't involve you having to get up and embarrass yourself by balancing on one leg or do a headstand against the wall. This is a discreet exercise. It can be done quietly whether you are in an office, classroom, train or plane.

Activity 16: How to Stop Yawning and Start Thinking: 'Brain-wash'

By the end of this activity you and your child will:

★   Know how to switch your brain from bored to alert in less than a couple of minutes.
★   Realize that when you focus you can harness the energy of your body and mind together – whenever you want to.

For this activity, you and your child will need:

♦   A chair each with a good back support that allows you to be able to place your feet flat on the floor and space enough to be able to put your arms close down the sides of your body;

♦   A pen or pencil, a piece of paper and a table;

♦   A glass of still fresh water.

Study the sketches on page 163 for each step above, then sit down on chairs that provide solid support for your backs. Place your feet flat on the floor. Bring your knees together, then your feet together. Keep your back straight and clench your buttocks together. Bring each of your hands down close to your sides so that they are holding the base of the chair. Now let your hands clench the chair, still keeping a straight back (not tense, just nice and straight). Now nestle your buttocks into the back of the chair. Clench everything together firmly at the same time: feet, knees and buttocks, with hands clenching the chair. Hold it for a count of 10 seconds and then relax, exhale and take a deep breath. Exhale again softly. Well done. Take a drink of your glass of water, don't gulp, just sip. Then take your pencil and paper. Using the opposite hand that you normally write with, try and write your name. Well done! To celebrate, finish the rest of your water!

[Note: while this is a very simple and easy exercise to do while sitting down, if you or your child have sustained a back injury or injuries of any nature which may prevent you from being able to do this, then I recommend that you check with a medical practitioner first.]

Energy booster for the brain

When I do the brain-wash in seminars, and people are trying it out for the first time, it usually raises a few laughs. That's fine – it's one of the reasons I do it! Laughing changes our state of mind, gets the blood pumping and our brains working again. If we find ourselves in a situation where we have had to sit still for 20 minutes or longer and are gradually going comatose, a brainwash is extremely refreshing!

How to Switch Your Mind from 'Screensaver' to Full Systems Go!

When we do this exercise we give our brains an instant energy boost. How is this? As we all know the first thing that happens when we get bored or sleepy is that we start to yawn. Obviously, yawning specifically involves our jaws, rather than, say, an involuntary waving of our left arm. This is because the jaw muscles are the easiest thing the brain can manipulate to get an energy boost. At its most basic, yawning is a result of the brain saying: '*Hello! Is there anybody there? I'm getting a little low on the old energy supply up here. Is there any way you can give me an energy booster?*' The quickest way to give our brains a help here is to pump blood up and around our head by squeezing our jaw muscles together. Only the brain knows when it has satisfied its energy needs. This is why when we start yawning, we just keep on going (no matter how embarrassing the situation!), depending upon how much boosting the brain decides is required. Stifling a yawn doesn't help either, because the brain is still sending messages down that it needs energy.

This exercise enables us to take control of the situation, and at the same time it gives our brains a better booster. It works because it uses not just a small group of muscles in our jaws, but major muscle groups in our whole body to give our minds and bodies a physiological jump start. By cramping up the muscles from top to toe and then releasing them, exhaling and inhaling and exhaling again, we give ourselves a mini workout which:

♦   Instantly gets the blood pumping around;
♦   Gives a boost to our body's whole circulation;
♦   Increases our oxygen uptake;
♦   Feeds the brain with energy.

Having a glass of water made sure that our bodies and minds were not dehydrated, to ensure concentration is working at its maximum.

OK, but what about having to write our names using the hand we don't normally use for writing? What was all that about? Remember the left–right brain activity your child did earlier in this section in which they learnt that the left hemisphere of the brain is associated with writing. For reasons not yet fully understood, if the *left* hemisphere does the mental activity involved in writing, it is our *right* hand that carries out the physical activity of writing. If, as we saw earlier, we are left-handed then the right hemisphere is the one most likely to be doing the mental activity involved in writing. By switching hands we were making our brains wake up, because they had to do some serious thinking to achieve what we ordinarily find easy. Suddenly the rules for the mental and physical activity of writing had been reversed. The brain is then taken out of its comfort zone, and has to figure out what to do in this situation. Result: in combination with all the other exercise we did in this activity, we changed our state from a drowsy one to a 'hey, what's this?' alert one, and so we are able to keep awake in a meeting for example. But, of course, there is one thing this exercise cannot do for you, and that is to ensure the meeting you are in is not going to be boring! Such is life …

CHECKPOINT

Q: **What do I do if my child constantly complains of being bored at school?**

A: **We have all come across children flopped full-length on the sofa, with half a bag of cookies, the TV control in one hand, and their mobile in the other, calling a friend to say – in the way that only children can – 'I'm bored!' We have all felt like this at some time or another. But if your child is frequently bored at school, and this is causing them stress, anger or even resentment, then it can be a strong indicator that their individual creativity and abilities are not being challenged or engaged. This is fully discussed in chapter 3. If you have yet to read this chapter, now is a good time to flick back there so that you can work out a plan to nip this problem in the bud.**

FAQs

☼   **Q:** What about the relationship between brain and diet?

☼   **A:** Just like our bodies, it is common sense that our brains require a balanced diet in order to function at their best. But mention 'diet' to any child in junior or high school and they will most likely think along the lines of low-fat foods that will help them keep a slim figure or toned physique like their favourite model, pop or film star. This is not your child's fault, of course. Every day they are bombarded with images of what they supposedly *should* look like physically. So successful have advertisers been in doing this that it is as if children have the 'perfect physique and figure' tattooed on their brains. If you ask a child whether they know the kind of diet that might be good for their brains, understandably therefore they will probably draw a blank. All this is about to change. If the 20th century was all about our bodies, the 21st century is going to be about the mind. It is one of the next great frontiers in science and research, and the relationship between diet and food has noticeably exploded over the last decade.

☼   **Q:** Can we eat ourselves smarter?

☼   **A:** In order to answer this question accurately we first have to decide what we mean by smart and how we are going to measure it. You already know from chapter 2, that while there are a profusion of different kinds of ability tests, *there is no definitive test for what is smart and what is not.*

Testing for ability is one thing, but having a healthy diet to feed our brain as well as our body is another. Research into the relationship between diet and the brain has revealed the importance of certain oils for the cognitive development of babies and children. Our brains comprise approximately 60% fat, so it follows that getting the balance of fats in our diet correct is important for optimal brain function. Two oils in particular, DHA and AA, are important for brain development.

Oiling the wheels of our minds – smart food

DHA (docosahexaenoic acid) is a fatty acid that features naturally in a mother's breast milk. Scientists already knew by the 1990s that children who had been breastfed demonstrated a tendency to do better academically than children who had not. By breaking down the chemical make-up of breast milk, scientists have been investigating whether there was a particular ingredient in breast milk that helped children to develop not only improved cognitive ability but also better eyesight. From studies to date all indications are that DHA forms a major ingredient in this brain development.

But why is this oil so important for our brains? DHA helps to keep nerve cells physically fit, so that the communication between them is maintained at maximum efficiency. When they are operating at their best, nerve cells are able to fire signals and communicate with each other with great ease and speed. DHA oils the wheels of our brain's communication system. In this sense our brains are like a racing car – we need a top-grade engine oil to ensure that we always get optimum performance.

Why your grandma may have been a genius

Apart from breast milk what are the other natural sources of DHA? Over the last few years the benefits for our heart of Omega-3 fatty acids found in fish oils have come to light. DHA is one type of Omega-3 fatty acid that is found naturally in good supply in oily fish such as tuna, salmon and mackerel. So your grandma was probably right when she said that eating fish made you brighter.

AA (arachidonic acid) is another fatty acid which, like DHA, occurs naturally in breast milk and oily fish. It is particularly important in infancy, in conjunction with DHA, for the healthy development of vision, cognitive ability and the central nervous system. DHA and AA are now found regularly in baby formulas.

While both DHA and AA have been found to be important for healthy brain development in babies, research indicates that DHA may have a longer-term role in keeping our brain cells in tip-top condition. Current indications from research are that DHA has an extremely important role to play in maintaining our mental ability, as it is one of the oils found to be present constantly in normally functioning brain cells.

It goes without saying that we need to view all of this in perspective. Unless your child is on a specific type of diet for medical reasons, then including oily fish in their regular diet will ensure that their brain as well as their body is being kept in great shape. All of this is good for adults' brains as well.

Exercising yourself brighter

No matter what we are doing our brains must have a constant supply of energy from our bodies. Oxygenated blood enables the brain to function. So it follows that the quality of oxygenated blood that is fed to the brain will affect the condition it is kept in. Also, we all know that one of the main reasons we feel good about ourselves after exercise is that we have 'downloaded' lots of mental stress. At the same time, chemicals known as endorphins, our body's own natural 'feel good' boosters, are released. We feel positive and ready for anything. Combining a balanced diet with regular exercise is just as important for our minds as it is for our bodies, as it keeps the flow of freshly oxygenated blood pumping into our brains.

If your child is not doing any kind of exercise at the moment then that needs changing. There is an old Far Eastern saying that what we learn at eight stays with us until we are eighty. You and I know that getting into the habit of doing regular exercise and eating a balanced diet will benefit their mind as well as their body for the whole of their life. If you and your child are already involved in regular exercise activity – well done you! On the other hand, if either of you are in danger of slowly growing into the sofa, the following case study will give you some instant inspiration.

Smart mice go jogging

Neuroscientists at the Salk Institute in the USA have recently discovered that the benefits to the mind from exercise may be more than just good for stress reduction and fat-busting – exercise may actually help to make us smarter. Laboratory tests on mice were conducted over a five-week period. One group of mice were put on a regime of exercise, three hours a day. The other group of mice were given a more sedentary existence, free of any regular exercise. At the end of the study it was found that stronger connectivity had developed between the brain cells of the mice that had exercised. In other words, the jogger mice were smarter than the sedentary ones!

When I relate this finding to people, it is not unusual to see them smiling quietly to themselves as they imagine little white mice lifting weights, working out on the rowing machine, and jogging off down the road, while their friends sit on the sofa flicking between TV channels! But if you can just let go that image for a moment, the findings of this study are important in understanding just how important exercise is in getting the best out of our minds as well as our bodies.

Mozart, music and intelligence

In 1993 researchers at the University of California generated huge media interest. They had conducted an experiment to see if playing Mozart to people before they took an ability test might improve their score. It did! The logical explanation is that Mozart's music acts as a kind of mental warm-up for the brain, making it ready to deal with the kinds of thinking and reasoning involved in mathematics or analytical problems. But the question remains to be answered whether the effect is only short term or whether listening to Mozart actually causes lasting changes inside the brain that could increase a child's intelligence over time.

None of us should view the connection between music and the mind as surprising in any way. We have all been moved to tears or joy by a piece of music. On other days we might notice that we are simply not in the mood for any kind of music and just want to switch the CD player off and enjoy the quiet! Our minds are constantly open to and affected by all kinds of external stimuli – music is just one of them.

Something else may have occurred to you to at this point. Earlier in this section, you learned that we use emotion and reasoning in our learning and that the limbic system is the mixing unit that brings these two together in our brain. Might playing music help the limbic system do its job better somehow? While we are asking ourselves these questions today, the idea that specifically music and thinking should be linked is nothing new. Einstein sometimes played Mozart on his violin when he was working an idea or problem through. In the 5th and 6th centuries the Greek philosopher and mathematician, Pythagoras, successfully brought together the study of geometry and music by arguing that they were all linked.

A holistic diet for learning

All of the matters we have discussed with regard to the brain in this and the previous chapter, indicate the best way to think about our brains is not as though different parts of it were working in isolation from other parts, but holistically. Viewed in this way, a *balanced* diet is the key for optimum brain function, whether we are talking about basic brain maintenance, or thinking and learning. Listening to Mozart may help us think from time to time; eating mackerel is good for body and brain, as is exercise; but if your child listened to Mozart 14 hours each day, did 10 hours on the trampoline, and ate nothing but water and mackerel (DHA) for 365 days of the year, it wouldn't do them any good. More worrying, is that they might end up being transformed into an extremely bouncy musical fish!

In order to get the best out of our brain in our thinking and learning, it requires that we give it a balanced diet not only of food and exercise, but also that we strive at every opportunity to work with its own natural system of processing information. Our brains are built to learn using every range of sense available to it, from the sensitivity of our fingertips, taste buds and nose, to listening to people talking, seeing pictures, watching others and hearing songs on the radio.

How many times have you driven through a busy city, stopping at crossroads, dodging traffic, listening to a hit song on the radio, while thinking through a problem? At the end of the drive you will have solved the problem, learned the words of the new song, whether you wanted to or not (because it involved rhythm and both sides of your brain), and remembered the finer details of a new sports car you spotted on the way. And yet when it comes to 'learning' we forget about all this natural learning ability and try and follow one way we were taught at school, or by a friend, sibling or parent. Maybe that works for us, maybe it doesn't. Either way, we carry on in the only way we know how, without discovering whether we could improve on our learning.

Whatever else learning is, in its most natural brain state, it is a multi-sensory and highly individualized activity. And because we are all so very individual, no one learning theory, no one way of doing things is going to work for everyone, least of all for your child. Study the lives of da Vinci, Einstein and Mozart, and you will find that they had figured this out. They identified their individual gifts, took that as their starting point, and then tailored their learning pattern to suit *their* own needs. Chapter 9 shows children how to do this for themselves.

But before we move on, the following activity will enable children to understand for themselves the importance of a balanced diet in keeping their brains in tip-top condition.

Activity 17: Ways to Keep Your Magic Mind in Shape

In this quick quiz, children have to try and guess the correct answer to each question. When they have finished the quiz, discuss each topic with them, and how each is important, in moderation, for keeping their brain in shape.

By the end of this activity, your child will have learned:

★   More key facts about how their brain works;
★   How to maintain their brain in tip-top condition.

QUIZ QUESTIONS
1   Physical exercise is good for your brain as well as your body. *True or False?*
2   Our brain is 60% fat. *True or False?*
3   Tuna, salmon and mackerel are all good brain food because they contain special oils that our brain needs to work brilliantly every day. *True or False?*
4   Our brains are like a fast sports car! They need top-grade oils to perform at their best. *True or False?*

5   A balanced diet is good for our brains as well as our butt. *True or False?*
6   Listening to Mozart's music can help us to think. *True or False?*
7   Our brain learns using all its senses. *True or False?*
8   What are the names of the five senses our brain uses to learn with?

[*The answers are given at the end of the chapter*]

Grey matter – Hollywood's hidden talent

If your child is not yet convinced that it is cool to pay as much attention to their grey matter as the way they look, then some home truths about the brain power of five glamorous Hollywood celebrities might help to change their mind. All of the following actors and actresses have used their brains as well as their looks to achieve their success. Each one is a film star *and* a graduate of a prestigious Ivy League university in the USA.

•   Reese Witherspoon, alias the blonde legal genius Elle Woods in the film *Legally Blonde*, graduated Stanford University.
•   Natalie Portman, alias the brave, beautiful and clever Queen Amidala in *Star Wars: The Phantom Menace*, graduated Harvard University.
•   Tommy Lee Jones, alias the *Men in Black* comedy star, graduated Harvard University.
•   David Duchovny, alias agent Fox Mulder in the *X Files*, graduated Yale University.
•   Jodie Foster, Oscar winner, director, producer, and star of *Panic Room* and *Silence of the Lambs*, graduated Yale University.

OK, so none of these stars have yet decided to pursue a career in academia. But there is absolutely no evidence to suggest that acting is any less demanding on their brain than would be a career in academia! The point here is that their brain, as well as how they look, has been a part of the journey that has enabled them to achieve what they have in their careers. There is another positive message for your child from all of this. If these people can develop and explore the *full range* of their different talents and gifts like this, then so can they.

Brainbox

- ① DHA is an Omega-3 fatty acid that scientists believe helps keep the brain's communication system working in tip-top condition.

- ① The brain is 60% fat so it follows that fatty acids should have an important role to play in maintaining good brain function.

- ① Physical exercise not only keeps our bodies in shape it helps stimulate our brains.

- ① In the 1990s researchers in the USA carried out an experiment to see if playing Mozart's music to people might help them improve their scores on standard ability tests. It did!

- ① We can switch our minds from being drowsy to alert using the 'brain-wash' exercise.

- ① The 'brain-wash' is a discreet mental and physical exercise which can be done while sitting down. It uses major muscle groups and left–right brain thinking to give the brain an energy boost.

- ① Whatever else learning is, in its most natural brain state, it is both a multi-sensory and highly individualized process.

- ① Due to the highly visual world we live in, our children can be forgiven for thinking that their body rather than brains is the fast route to fame and fortune! A few familiar faces in this chapter helped to show your child that this stereotype does not ring true – brains as well as looks have helped these stars to achieve their success.

[Answers to Activity 17 – 1: True, 2: True, 3: True, 4: True, 5: True, 6: True, 7: True 8: taste, touch, sight, sound, smell.]

Chapter 9

Thumb Print Learning®

Learning like a genius

Learning, thinking and creativity went together for Mozart, Einstein and da Vinci. They found a way to learn which made the most of their natural abilities to question and think creatively. How did they achieve this? At different points in their lives they each recognized their own individual gifts and then took charge of their own learning to develop them. Our children can do this for themselves – when they know how. The trouble is, they either never have the knowledge or the opportunity to be able to do this.

Well now they can! Every child who has reached this chapter with their parent knows more about their brain, how it works, how they think and learn, and how to unlock their creativity than any past genius could ever have. Every child now knows that they have within them, not only their own individual gifts, but also the natural ability to combine their learning, thinking and creativity. What they have is all the knowledge they need to be able to tailor-make a learning system that suits them, and is as unique to them as their own thumb print. All they need is the chance to start developing that learning system for themselves, and that is what this chapter is all about. They are going to learn how to do this next.

5 Steps to Thumb Print Learning®

1 Taking charge of their own learning

The first step to take charge of their learning is for children to come face to face with the gifts they possess. This means recognizing and identifying what their gifts are. Some gifts will be more obvious than others. Remember the wide diversity of gifts we discussed in chapter 3. Any one or combination of them was an indication that a child may not only be gifted in, but had the potential to be, outstanding in a particular area. Remember too that children's gifts merge with each other rather than neatly fall into any one prescribed profile. Why should it be otherwise? Every child is an original!

Activity 18: My Special Gifts

How to help children get the best out of this activity

As you go through the following activity with children, the idea is not to try and pigeon-hole their abilities, but to let them see the full range of their gifts. Ask them to place a tick in the boxes that best identifies what they feel they are good at. Do not be put off by the fact that some of the descriptions are about subjects whilst others seem more general. This is purposeful and based on what you learned about discovering children's gifts in section II. Children's gifts come in all kinds of wrapping, and can be masked. We have already seen how a child's tendency to be mischievous in lessons could mean that they are a quick thinker and/or easily get bored. Going through the list and ticking the boxes together is the best way forward here. Two heads are better than one when it comes to discussing our gifts. We do not always find it easy to blow our own trumpet about what we are good at, and other people can often see gifts that we cannot. At the same time, we do not always stop to think about what we are good at and it can often be a revelation when we do.

Don't see the list as exhaustive. If you or your child think of something that does not quite fall into any one of the descriptions, then by all means don't hesitate, add it to the list! This activity is about finding out what *your* child is good at, not another one size fits all theory that they must somehow squash into. Let rip, this is the opportunity to think about and get all of their gifts out into the open.

leading	designing ☐	☐
acting	independent thinker ☐	☐
dancing	ideas person ☐	☐
creative writing	imaginative ☐	☐
mature vocabulary	singing ☐	☐
team player	likes challenges ☐	☐
mathematical	reading ☐	☐
competitive sports	enjoys puzzles ☐	☐
solitary sports	art ☐	☐
music	languages ☐	☐
history	high energy level ☐	☐
technology/computing	quick thinker ☐	☐
geography	practical ☐	☐
sciences ☐		

Afterward discuss the range of gifts that you have identified together. Do a double check to make sure that you both have not missed any, you are happy with your choices, and add anything extra to the list if you need to.

Then, for each one you have ticked or listed, jot down an example of how your child demonstrates this gift. For example if you ticked 'likes challenges' – that could manifest itself in the fact that they enjoy homework that makes them think and work hard to find something out for themselves.

Alternatively, it could manifest itself in volunteering to go on an outdoor pursuit course at school. In each case, let children make the list their own, by adding in all the personal details that show what their special gifts are.

2 Harness learning opportunities

Now that you and your child have identified their gifts, the next step is to let them harness every learning opportunity, and map out how their gifts can be developed best using the resources available to them. You and your child need to think:

♦   What opportunities are there inside school?
♦   Are there any opportunities outside school?
♦   Are there any problems that need ironing out?
♦   What are the solutions that could be worked out?

Activity 19: Mapping Out Opportunities

How to help children get the best out of this activity

This activity works around the four questions above. It enables your child to think about the learning opportunities available to them, and how they can harness these to develop their own individual gifts and interests. It also offers you both the chance to iron out any niggling problems at school. For example, your child may have the opportunity to take part in a learning activity in school that their friends aren't really interested in. Brainstorming the pros and cons of taking part in the activity will help them map out a solution that will work for them, and that they are happy with.

Watch out for too eager beavers! Harnessing learning opportunities is brilliant, overdoing it is not. As they do this activity, it is natural that children can get carried away and want to try a whole load of different learning activities. That is fine as long as they remember what they have learned here: 'think time' is just as important as 'learn time'. Trying to pack too much into their day, week or semester will just leave them feeling drained. No matter how high their energy level is they need time to chill out and relax! A good plan is a balanced one. Make sure they have thought about this when they are discussing options with you and mapping out what they would like to do. Remind them they can still develop their gifts alongside their other subjects at school – and enjoy a healthy social life too!

A word to the wise

It goes without saying that you may have some great ideas about activities your child could explore to develop their gifts. For example, you may have heard of a good summer school from a friend and be bubbling with enthusiasm as any caring parent would. But as we all know, if a child does not want to go, and you yield to the temptation to pack them off anyway, they will never let you forget it if they do not enjoy themselves. Thumb Print Learning® puts the ball in their court. It empowers them with all the knowledge they need to make informed decisions and choices, and at the same time it takes away all the angst of trying to think for them. By talking ideas through with them, we get *them* thinking through different options for themselves. Who knows, a few weeks later they may surprise you either by deciding that they would like to give your idea a go, or coming up with another even better idea of their own. Either way you both win and are still friends!

Opportunities inside school	Opportunities outside school
Problems:	
Solutions:	

Once they have discussed everything with you, and you have hammered out a plan together, your child will have begun not only to learn how to take charge of their own learning; they will also be able to move forward with real confidence. They will know where they are going and how they are going to get there. But remember, a plan for this week, month, term or year is only good for that time frame. Circumstances can change and regularly reviewing the plan will ensure that it is always fresh and relevant to their individual needs and gifts.

All that remains now is for them to know how to maximize each learning opportunity. They can do this by bringing together all that they have learned so far about their brain, and the natural thinking and learning abilities they possess.

3 Use the mind's own natural theory of learning

As they worked through all the activities they did in each of the chapters, children discovered that they have a brilliant brain, and that it learns using the following natural abilities:

- ◆ Emotion (happy learning is effective learning);
- ◆ Multi-senses (our brains use all five senses to learn);
- ◆ Curiosity (questioning: 'Why Tree');
- ◆ Creativity (ideas and imagination: 'What if?' 'Why not?').

When they learn to use these natural abilities together they are using their brain's own natural theory of learning:

$$E + M + C^2 = Smart$$

Your child first discovered each of these natural learning abilities separately. Now they are going to have the opportunity to see how smart learning works. They will see how when they use all of these natural abilities together, learning can be both effective and enjoyable. Each of the following activities show children how to use their emotion, senses, natural curiosity and creativity to take charge of information and make it their own.

Activity 20: I'm a Clever Cat!

In this activity children discover that learning facts becomes easier when they learn how to present information to themselves in a more user-friendly format. When they learn how to do this, their minds can find a way into the information and learn quicker. Knowing how to do this not only helps children learn better, it builds their self-confidence and frees up their natural curiosity to explore the topic for themselves. This activity teaches your child how to do this using the following strategies:

★   Rhyme and Rhythm;
★   Imagery;
★   Humour;
★   Questioning.

How to help children get the best out of this activity

This activity can be done anywhere – a family trip on the train, plane or at home – it really doesn't matter. The same principles apply whether a child is in junior or high school. All they will need is some coloured pencils and paper.

Invite your child to look at the 'I'm a clever cat' illustration on page 183. On the left hand side of the tiger are a lot of unconnected facts about tigers. Underneath the tiger, the information has been made much more user-friendly; it engages different senses and ideas. There is a rhyme about all the facts about tigers. At the side of each verse of the rhyme wacky pictures reinforce the facts to be learned. All of this makes the learning experience into a livelier and more memorable one. 'Dull facts' are transformed into 'fun facts'. But the learning about tigers doesn't stop there. There is more to explore and learn about them, and questions that children may want to ask about them. By encouraging children to use their natural curiosity to learn,

I'm a Clever Cat!

Panthera Tigris

Can live happily in either cold conditions or hot jungles.
Whether they are male or female they use their tails for balance.
Their paw prints have a special name they are called pug marks.
A tiger's night vision is six times better than a human's.

 × **6**   Six times better sight,
Than people at night!

 Balances with its tail.
Male or female!

 Cold places or hot
Bothers a tiger not!

 'Pug' prints 'paw' prints – not the same!
'Cos *Panthera Tigris* is my name!

Question: Where might you find tigers in the world?

and their ability to think independently, they are invited to find out more about tigers for themselves, and/or to make connections between the clues they are given in the verse.

Give your child a chance to really explore the picture and find out all about tigers. Then let them practice making 'dull facts into fun facts' for themselves using the following information about kangaroos and by following the four steps below.

All about Kangaroos

- Females are called 'flyers' and males are called 'boomers';
- Baby kangaroos are called 'joeys';
- Male kangaroos don't have pouches;
- Female kangaroos do have pouches;
- A kangaroo can hop at speed of up to 40 miles per hour (60 km per hour);
- A group of kangaroos is called a 'mob'.

Step 1: Start by drawing a funny picture of a kangaroo – the funnier the better!

Step 2: Now take charge of the facts. List them under different headings: 'males', 'females', 'babies', 'kangaroo groups' and 'travel speed'. Then make these facts into a little rhyme for yourself.

Step 3: Next to each of the verses draw a picture that reminds you of the key points – the funnier the better!

Step 4: Ask yourself: *'How did kangaroos get their name?'*

The last activity enabled your child to learn a set of facts about something. The next activity focuses on how to learn about more abstract concepts. How did geniuses do it?

Draw – like a genius!

Take a look at the writings of 'geniuses' and you will see that more often than not they have used quick sketches and drawings to work their ideas and thoughts through for themselves. Einstein and da Vinci's works, for example, are littered with sketches and drawings that they used to help them work out solutions to problems or visualize abstract concepts. When we are toddlers we often use pictures to help us to learn, but, as we get older, using pictures and sketches falls by the wayside as we learn to write or type, – as though these kinds of activities are somehow superior tools in our learning. In reality, visualizing abstract concepts using sketches is one trick of genius that should not be missed! It is so easy and effective to use and it works. The next activity shows your child how.

Activity 21: Einstein's Theory of Relativity Made Simple!

In this activity children will learn the following strategies to enable them to learn abstract concepts better and faster. They will learn how to:

★   Break down abstract concepts;
★   Make them friendlier;
★   Visualize them to simplify them;
★   Use their natural curiosity to understand them.

Using these strategies, in this activity your child will find their own way into two basic concepts that underpin the first part of Einstein's theory of relativity: the speed of light is the only thing that is constant in the universe. Therefore, wherever we are and whatever we are doing, the speed of light is always the same.

Relativity Made Simple

Albert Einstein
(1879–1955)

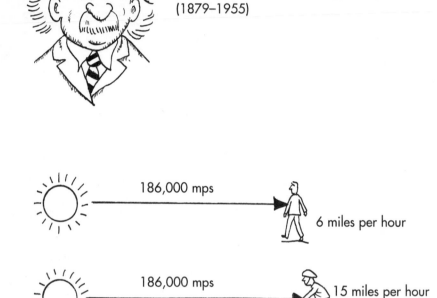

- Einstein's theory says that light travels at 186,000 miles per second.
- Wherever we are and whatever we are doing, the speed of light always remains the same.

Question: Which kind of science was Einstein an expert in?

How does this happen in practice? Imagine two Ferraris travelling toward each other at exactly the same speed of 100 miles per hour: at the moment they pass each other they will do so at a relative speed of 200 miles per hour. But if we replace one of the Ferraris with a beam of light, this rule breaks down. No matter how fast the sports car travels toward the beam of light, it will always hit it at the same speed. If we are able to visualize all of this, the concept becomes much easier to appreciate and understand. And that is the whole purpose of this activity.

Why choose the theory of relativity?

At this point you may wonder why we should introduce children to such a famously complex scientific concept with this activity! The reason is simple. Throughout school your child encounters topics which because they are new or abstract, sound complex. But then, as we saw in chapter 5, simple tasks such as riding a bike are extremely complex when we don't know how to do them! Yet our children manage to accomplish them – no problem! Why? They have seen it can be done, and their expectation is that they will be able to do so as well. As we saw in chapter 2, our children do not know something is complex until we tell them that it is and put them right off by saying: '*Oh no! Don't try that! It's really too complex*'.

In formal learning situations it is not always possible for children to see that someone else has learned what they are trying to learn, because all their peers are in the same boat of being absolute beginners. Without the individual learning tools to deal with, and master new knowledge of any kind, they are therefore solely dependent on others to figure it out. If after asking their teacher they are still not 100% sure about something, left to their own devices children will then do one of three things reminiscent of contestant behaviour on a televized quiz show. They will either stoically battle it out, try bravely to sort it out by trial and error, or ask a friend to try and explain it. If they are feeling particularly at a loss about a topic they can be tempted just to give up on themselves. That is how not to think like a genius!

Instead, with a range of smart learning strategies 'up their sleeve,' children can be ready for anything! Immediately they know how to break down the new information into something manageable that they can understand for themselves. Now they are beginning to think like a genius!

How to help children get the best out of this activity

Let them explore the illustration 'Relativity Made Simple!' The principal concepts have been put in an image so that they can be visualized. Underneath the image the principal concepts have also been given in bulleted form. There is then one question for children to explore for *themselves*. No matter what age your child is, if they want to learn more about Einstein or the theory of relativity, then let them explore! Remember that age is no barrier to learning.

Once children have had a chance to explore and discuss the information in this activity, they can practise using the same strategy for themselves for another abstract concept, Newton's Laws of Motion, following the steps as given below.

Step 1: Read the following story:

> *The Apple Tree*
> Ever wondered why when you drop something it falls straight to the ground? In the 16th and 17th centuries, Sir Isaac Newton wondered the same thing. Legend has it that he was out walking one day and saw an apple fall from a tree to the ground. It got him thinking: '*Why did the apple do that? Why did it fall in a straight line to the ground. Why didn't it zigzag a bit and then fall?*' After thinking about it Newton realized that all objects are either 'at rest' (like an apple in a tree) or moving. And when an

object moves (like an apple falling from a tree) it moves at a constant (fixed) speed, and in a straight line – unless something forces it not to.

Step 2: Draw a quick sketch of an apple smiling 'at rest' in a tree.

Step 3: Now sketch an apple frowning as it falls from the tree to the ground. Draw an arrow in a straight line showing the apple's path from the tree straight down to the ground.

Step 4: Next to or underneath your two sketches write the following: Newton's law says an object moves:

♦ at a constant speed;
♦ in a straight line, unless something forces it not to.

Step 5: Now question this law for yourself. Think about it, what happens when a football is thrown into the air? It drops straight back down unless we kick it, head it, or if it is blown by the wind. These forces will change its speed and direction.

Feel it, be it, learn it!

If you have ever had to learn a new language you will know that it can be a bit daunting – when you do not know how to approach it. At the same time, you can come back from holiday abroad and find yourself singing a pop song in an entirely foreign language. You do not know *what* you are singing, but you remember it! And every time you sing it, all the good times come back to you to. There are three reasons why this learning happens so easily. Knowing from earlier chapters how the brain and memory works you can probably guess them for yourself.

1   When you choose to go abroad for your holiday, you *expect* new experiences, including language, food, music and culture. Your

mind's natural curiosity is therefore awake to look out for and learn new things.

2   When you hear a song, just like any other song, no matter what language it is in, there will be a melody and words, so your left–right brain connectivity is instantly buzzing.

3   You have a *context*. In other words, even though the song may be a bunch of jumbled up foreign words that you do not actually understand, it still means something to you: a happy experience. Hence, your mind can personalize and make alive the information by associating it with something familiar that it understands – a holiday.

Just like all the other strategies in these activities, children can learn how to tap into this relaxed and natural way of learning on demand.

Activity 22: Hieroglyphs? Piece of Cake!

In this next activity your child is going to learn how to use four strategies to recreate this state of mind for learning new information – *without* having to go on holiday:

★   Music;
★   Mime;
★   Context;
★   Curiosity.

When children or adults begin to experiment with the strategies used in this activity they usually start by laughing, because at first they feel a bit silly. It is great when this happens, because it means that already their minds are getting into a relaxed and open state and ready to learn something new.

The activity purposely focuses upon a language in which few readers are likely to be fluent – ancient Egyptian hieroglyphs. The reason for this is to give children a clear and confidence-building message: if they can learn *this language*, using these strategies, then obviously they can use them again to learn anything!

In the illustration on page 192 they will see three Egyptian hieroglyphs. If they have never seen them before children will be able figure out where the language comes from by the images used in the picture. By using mime and music they are going to put these unfamiliar symbols into a more familiar context, and in the process discover another way to help them tap into their natural ability to learn and master knew knowledge. They are then invited to use their own thinking and curiosity to find out more about the language and country before they finish the activity.

How to help children get the best out of this activity

Let them look at the illustration. If they want to, let them try and find out more about hieroglyphs before they do the language-learning activity. Then, as soon as they are ready, all they have to do is follow the steps below.

Step 1: Look at each of the Egyptian hieroglyph letters for 'h', 'b' and 'm'.
Step 2: Now, look at each one as you say to yourself:

♦ ' "h" is a house and it looks like this': using your finger to draw out the shape of the symbol in the air;
♦ ' "b" is like a boot and it looks like this': pull on an imaginary boot;
♦ ' "m" is like an owl and it looks like this': make your fingers and thumbs into two large circles round your eyes to mimic the shape of an 'm' and the eyes of an owl;

Hieroglyphs? Piece of Cake!

Ancient Egyptians used hieroglyphs to write.
Here are three letters from their alphabet.

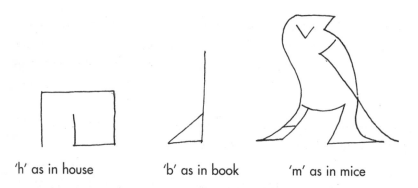

'h' as in house   'b' as in book   'm' as in mice

Questions:

♦   Where is Egypt?
♦   Do you think that writing in pictures like this is a good idea?

♦ End by saying to yourself: '*These three letters I have learned today!*'

Step 3: Now repeat Step 2, doing everything to the tune of *Twinkle, Twinkle Little Star*, or if you like you can try it to the tune of your favourite pop song.

Step 4: Speed it up, do the whole thing as fast you can, and then without looking at the picture, write down the three letters you have learned.

Next time your child feels they are faced with a mountain of new knowledge, and are perhaps feeling a bit overwhelmed – be it learning a language or any other subject – remind them of what they did in this activity. Using the strategies here will immediately enable them to familiarize whatever it is, shrink it down to size and master it! All by using their natural thinking and learning abilities.

4 Making changes to suit them as and when they need to

To get the best out of these strategies children need to experiment with them and apply them to new topics and learning situations as often as they can. The more they do this, the more your child *makes them their own*. But it doesn't end there. Once they start to use these strategies they will find ways of adapting and changing them to suit *their* individual needs. This is Thumb Print Learning® in action. At this point children are not only taking charge of their learning, they are selecting and amending strategies to make their learning system unique to their own needs. Those needs will change as they encounter new learning experiences of their own, and with those experiences discover new gifts. At every turn, our children are growing and developing. They do not stand still and neither does their Thumb Print Learning®, it grows with them to take in new experiences and meet their changing needs as and when they happen.

5 Bringing their own ideas into their learning

As we saw at the beginning of this book, theories of learning for children have traditionally focused on preparing them for knowledge *gathering*, as opposed to knowledge *creation*. Einstein and da Vinci never knew this division. They managed to learn *and* create new knowledge naturally, and so can your child. From the minute they identify their own gifts, take charge of their learning, and start adapting the strategies they have learned here, they become awake to new possibilities. They may have ideas of their own as to how they can make their learning fun and effective, and I really hope they do. What they have started with here are the foundations of knowledge of how the human brain works, and how to maximize on their natural abilities for learning. But new knowledge about the brain, and how we think and learn is being created all the time. Thumb Print Learning® is not static, it is organic. It is not blind to new knowledge but embraces it. If a child learns something new about their brain, their learning and their thinking, they should feel free to experiment with that, and bring it into their Thumb Print Learning®. Who knows, in a few year's time it could be *your* child that has discovered something new about our brains or how we think and learn. Why not?

Activity 23: My Thumb Print Learning

When they have done all the activities in this chapter, they must celebrate themselves! The sensation for children of printing their own unique identity onto their own learning in the illustration on page 195, will remind them how unique and brilliant they really are. It will consolidate all that they have learned and discussed with you, and help them to remember that they have within them the ability to learn *whatever* they want, whenever they want. If they haven't done it already, let them go do that thumb print – now!

My Own Thumb Print Learning®

Signed . . . .

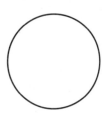

My thumb print

When I thumb print my
learning, I ...

Take charge of my learning

Harness all learning opportunites

Use my natural abilities to learn

Make changes to my learning when
I need to

Bring my own ideas into my learning

Preparing for Examinations

FAQ

 Q: How can my child best prepare for examinations?

A: They now have the ability to make learning easier for them when it comes to revision and examinations. They can apply all the strategies they have learned in this chapter to any knowledge they must revise. What they may not have is a strategy in place for examination preparation. This is because every examination will be different and require them to jump through different hoops. I call this the 90% strategy, 10% knowledge rule. Often a candidate can know a great deal but they approached the examination with the wrong strategy and scored less than they should have. Unfair I know but true. So here is a checklist which you can use to help children prepare best, and make sure all their hard work pays off.

Checklist: Strategies for examination success

✓   Q: *What precisely is the examiner looking for?*

✓   A: This may sound a stupid question, because no one can get inside an examiner's head. This is true but examiners for national or school examinations are usually following a syllabus. The trick is to find out what the criterion for success is. Most exam boards clearly print this information in their literature for examinations and you can ask your school to give you a copy. Some schools give this to children. Check whether your child has anything like this which gives them a clue about what is going to be expected of them. Without knowing this information children are pretty much shooting in the dark. As the cliché goes, if they do not know where they are going, they could end up somewhere else – and it will not be where they want to be. Get the target straight and they can have a good shot at hitting it. Once you have got your hands on a document that sets out the finer details of what the examiner is looking for, you and your child can take a very large luminous marker, highlight the key information, and they can pin it on their bedroom wall/notice board – anywhere that is prominent – so that they cannot lose sight of what it is they are aiming to do.

✓ **Q:** How is it marked?

✓ **A:** Again this probably sounds self-evident. However, examinations are not always marked in the same ways. How many marks a child gets can depend how much weighting was given to different sections of the examination and how well a child did in each one. Find out how the marks are weighted in the sections of the examination. Make sure your child knows and that they know exactly how they will be marked.

Some examinations are also 'negative marked'. This means that every time a child puts something down that is incorrect they lose a mark. Other examinations place the emphasis on finding out more about what a child does know, rather than what they do not, and give marks accordingly. It is well worth children knowing which kind of marking system they are going to be dealing with.

✓ **Q:** *What is the focus of the examination?*

✓ **A:** Some subject examinations focus on a child knowing a certain topic inside out. Others are looking not so much for a child to have an in-depth knowledge of any one particular topic as much as understanding the connections between lots of topics on a syllabus. Going into their revision plan blindly about this can lead children to do a lot of work revising topics in isolation. When they sit the exam they will be able to write, and will write (because that is all they know), copious amounts about a topic, but not get the high marks they deserve because it was the relationships between topics that got candidates the best marks. This takes us back to the 90% strategy, 10% knowledge rule. Of course a child has to know a lot more about their topic than 10%. However, it will not do them any good whatsoever if they have 110% knowledge, and they do not know how to apply it, or what they get the best marks for. If they do a little detective work and find out what they get the highest marks for, not only will they do well, they will save themselves hours of unnecessarily slogging away at learning material they do not need to.

Children are quick learners, once they understand the answers to the three questions above in full, they will never forget to find out this level of detail about examinations in the future. Once they do that, they have taken charge of the situation, and are ready to attack the examination fully armed. Examinations become an opportunity to show what they can do, not something to fear. They expect success.

Expecting success

This last point cannot be underestimated. The state of mind in which children approach examinations can have an effect on how well they do, not just because they may get nervous, but because they have never had the opportunity to learn how to use their mind to put them in the mind-set for success. Before Einstein wrote his theory of relativity he visualized it, he saw it as if had already proven it. Our ability to do this is absolutely natural. Before a major event we may have certain expectations about how that event will go because it is important to us. Let's go back to our holidays again. When we book a holiday we expect what it is going to be like before we get there. We expect to enjoy ourselves! Even if everything is not exactly as we thought it might be when we arrive, we are determined to enjoy ourselves and 9 times out of 10 we do. If children expect to be phased out by an examination they are literally setting their mind up for failure. The next activity shows them how to use their natural mind's eye to see and expect success ahead. By expecting to pass, by seeing a picture of success, the brain starts to believe it and to put its own strategies in place to achieve it. You have heard the phrase *plant the seed of thought*. The same principle applies: once our mind knows what is possible or gets an idea, it works to achieve it. In fact, this process is as ancient as humankind itself. The following activity will help children harness this natural ability and use it to their advantage.

Activity 24: Winning!

How to help children get the best out of this activity

In this activity first ask them to sit comfortably on the sofa or chair. Then ask them to close their eyes. You will then guide them through a series of steps to create a picture in their mind's eye. Make sure you are both relaxed, their eyes are closed and you can begin, reading out the following steps of instructions to them:

Step 1: Choose a topic or subject area in which you would like to do really well.

Step 2: Now decide what it is exactly that you want to achieve (make sure you are precise about this, for example thinking about exam success, phrases such as '*top marks*', or '*a pass*', will not do. '*A pass with 75% on my science test*' is more like it).

Step 3: Now keeping your eyes closed picture the day that you achieve that goal. Do this with as detailed and colourful a picture as possible.

◆ Where are you when you achieve your goal?
◆ What are you wearing?
◆ Who are you with?
◆ Bring the picture to life with sights and sounds of the moment.
◆ Zoom into the picture now so that you can see yourself smiling, happy and people congratulating you on your success.

Step 4: Hold that picture for a few seconds, keep holding it and take a deep breath and exhale slowly. Smile to yourself at how well you have done.

Step 5: Now, keeping that smile and picture in your head, open your eyes again. Well done!

Regularly visualizing their success, as well as using what they have learned here to help them achieve it, enables children to see and believe they can do it. As they encounter new hurdles and leap over them, remind them to celebrate every win they have, the little ones as well as the big ones (they *all* count), and give themselves a pat on the back for being absolutely brilliant and a job well done.

Brainbox

① Existing learning theories for children focus on *knowledge gathering* as opposed to *knowledge creation*; Mozart, Einstein and da Vinci managed to do both.

① By taking charge of their own learning Mozart, da Vinci and Einstein brought their learning, thinking and creativity together.

① Thumb Print Learning® enables children to do this for themselves, beginning with identifying their own gifts.

- ① All children share natural thinking and learning abilities. At the same time they each have their own individual gifts.
- ① Thumb Print Learning® enables children to tailor-make their own learning.
- ① It puts smart knowledge at their fingertips, and their thinking and learning development in the best hands possible – *their own*!

Putting the Smart Knowledge for Learning in Their Own Hands

Make their
learning fun

Ask questions to
help them learn

Remember their
mind is magic

Select strategies
that work for them

Think independently
and creatively

Farewell

Einstein has never been far from my mind as I wrote this book. Everyone knows him as a successful scientist and outstanding researcher in his field. But life was not always so smooth. He encountered one of the first setbacks in his life in his youth, when it was left up to other people (academics) to decide whether he had what it took to become a lecturer and researcher in science. They said he had not – *he proved he had*! Einstein's journey in life was full of twists and turns, just like everyone else's. *But he believed in himself.* He was not about to let someone else decide his future for him, and his letters to friends are a testament to that.

As I said at the beginning of the book, children live in a world that is currently peppered by tests, all claiming to be able to tell them what they are good at and wrap up their abilities in a neat and tidy bundle. If our children only ever learn how to sit tests, and leave it up to other people to tell them what they are capable of, their abilities and gifts will always be something that others decide for them. When I set out to write this book, I wanted to place at children's fingertips all the smart knowledge they needed to take charge of their own gifts, and develop their own thinking and learning; I wanted to put these precious and natural abilities that all children possess in the best hands possible – *their own*!

If after encountering what they have learned in these pages your child is fired up with the fact that the only *real* magic in this world is them, then I have succeeded in my aims. Before they reach for the stars, I would like every child to know how to discover the stars inside themselves. When they can see their own natural gifts and abilities, and how brilliant they are, you and I both know that even the sky is no limit for them.

Well, we are now at the end of this particular journey together, and I hate goodbyes. But for our children nothing is ending here, it is only a beginning. They stand each and every one of them, at the start of their own journeys, shining with their own individual gifts, dreams, ideas and thoughts – and I am rooting for all of them!

Fare *well*, I wish your children good health, happiness and every success. Now and always I hope they remember to believe in themselves, have faith in their abilities and, yes – go for it!

Where can I get information on ...?

Autism

Asperger's Syndrome: A Guide for Parents and Professionals by Tony Attwood, (Jessica Kingsley Publishers)

The Autistic Spectrum: A Guide for Parents and Professionals by Lorna Wing (Constable)

Emergence: Labelled Autistic, (Costello Publications) by Grandin Temple and Margaret M. Scariano is the inspirational story of a woman with autism who has successfully set up her own business, which she now runs.

Nobody Nowhere: The Remarkable Autobiography of an Autistic Girl and Somebody Somewhere: Breaking Free from the World of Autism (Transworld Publishers), both by Donna Williams, who lets us inside her life experience and helps us to try to understand what it is like to be a person with autism and succeed in living their life.

Charity

Beautiful Minds
Suite N1/17 Nortex Business Centre
Chorley Old Road
Bolton
England BL1 3AG

Beautiful Minds is dedicated to funding research into the best ways to develop the natural gifts of **all** children. The website contains details of the latest events, news and updates.

tel: + 44 (0) 1204 437123
fax: + 44 (0) 1204 845127
website: www.beautifulminds.co.uk

Dyslexia

Reading David: A Mother and Son's Journey Through the Labyrinth of Dyslexia by Lissa Weinstein and David Siever (Perigee Books) is about one family's experience with dyslexia.

How to Reach and Teach Children and Teens with Dyslexia: A Parent and Teacher Guide to Helping Students of All Ages Academically, Socially and Emotionally by Cynthia M. Stowe (Josey-Bass). A practical guide which makes clear different aspects of dyslexia.

Multiple Intelligences

See Howard Gardner's book *Frames of Mind*, (HarperCollins).

Problem-Solving Practice

Failure Is Not An Option by Gene Kranz (Berkeley) is a brilliant read as well as being packed with lessons in leadership, teamwork and problem-solving under pressure.

Mensa

The international high IQ society has numerous problem-solving activities and puzzles on-line. It also has special interest groups for children and details of testing centres in the UK with links to international centres.

website: www.mensa.org.uk

Imagine

Imagine is a magazine produced by children at the John Hopkins Center for Talented Youth containing inspirational stories of students, plus puzzles and games. It is available to order.

website: jhu.edu/gifted/imagine

Tests

Scholastic Attainment Tests

Used mainly (at present) in the UK and USA for university entrance and selection for acceleration programmes, alongside children's wider achievements and abilities. They comprise multiple choice questions over several sections that test verbal and mathematical reasoning. Find selections of them in Jerry Bobrow's *SAT I* (Cliffs Quick Review) and *SAT I Preparation Guide* (Cliffs Notes Inc).

World Class Arena and World Class Tests

World class tests were developed in conjunction with a range of countries around the world from the Middle East to Europe and America. The test is currently used by, and targeted at, parents and children in the UK. The tests are used by schools and national talent-spotting programmes, as well as summer school, enrichment and acceleration programmes, to assess thinking and problem-solving skills. They are available to parents on-line. Sample tests are available on their website.

website: www.worldclassarena.org

University programmes for acceleration, enrichment and summer schools

Australia

Gerric, School of Education,
University of New South Wales,
Sydney NSW 2052

Runs various programmes for gifted children throughout the year.

tel: + 61 2 9385 1972
fax: + 61 2 9385 1973
e-mail: wwwgerric@unsw.edu.au
website: unsw.edu.au

Asia Pacific Federation
Department of Education
Flinders University
Bedford Park, Australia 5042

website: www.flinders.edu.au

Canada

Centre for Gifted Education,
170 Education Block,
University of Calgary,
Alberta
Canada T2N 1N4

e-mail: gifteduc@acs.ucalgary.ca

Hong Kong

Hong Kong Acceleration Schools Project

website: www.fed.cuhk.edu.hk

Ireland

Irish Centre for Talented Youth,
Dublin City University
Dublin 9, Ireland

Runs programmes for different age ranges in a variety of subjects.

website: www.dcu.ie/ctyi

Middle East

Arab Council for the Gifted and Talented (ACGT)
PO Box 830578
Amman, Jordan 11163

At time of going to press ACGT was updating their information and website.

tel: 962-6-5238236
fax: 962-6-5234231
website: http://jubilee.edu.jo/english/links/web_pages/links_body

The Young Person's Institute for the Promotion of Creativity and Excellence (Tel Aviv)

The Institute was set up by Dr Erika Landau and provides workshops for children.

website: www.ypipce.org.il

New Zealand

Ministry of Education
PO Box 19098, Wellington

Their on-line learning centre, Te Kete Ipurangi, offers on-line curriculum materials for learning, help for primary students as well as various programmes for children.

tel: 64 4 8010462
fax: 64 4 3849317
website: www.tki.org.nz/r/gifted/talented/index_e.php

Singapore

Ministry of Education,
1 North Buona Vista Drive,
Singapore 138675

Offers a very comprehensive on-line menu of programmes, events and information for parents, including details of eEnrichment programmes, for both secondary and primary children, including summer camps in languages, creative writing, technology and mathematics, as well as leadership programmes for children.

tel: 68721110
fax: 67755826
website: www.moe.gov.sg/gifted/Enrichment_Activities

UK

The National Academy for Gifted and Talented Youth,
Warwick University,
Coventry, CV4 7AL

Details of intake for programmes, selection criteria, acceleration, enrichment and summer school programmes are available on their web site.

website: www.warwick.ac.uk/gifted

The University of York
Heslington, York YO 10 5DD

Offers summer schools, and extra-curricular subjects in a wide range of disciplines.

website: www.york.ac.uk/admin/uao

USA

Education Programme for Gifted Youth (EPGY),
Ventura Hall, Stanford University
Stanford, CA 94305 - 4115

Runs established programmes for children from kindergarten upward to university. Offers summer programmes catering for children from different countries.

website: www-epgy.stanford.edu/

John Hopkins Centre for Talented Youth
The John Hopkins University,
3400 North Charles Street
Baltimore, Maryland 21218

tel: (410) 516-0337
fax: (410) 516-0804/0108

Western Regional Centre for Talented Youth
Johns Hopkins University
4640 Admiralty Way, Suite 301
Marina Del Rey, CA 90292

tel: (310) 754-4100

Both the above centres run regular acceleration, enrichment and summer
programmes for children.

website: www.cty.jhu.edu/contact

Southern Methodist University
P.O. Box Dallas, Texas 75275

Offers various programmes for children throughout the year.

website: www.smu.edu/continuing_education/youth/index.asp

Yale University
Child Study Centre
230 South Frontage Road
New Haven, CT 06520

Runs sports, art, dance, theatre and a wide variety of other programmes for children.

website: www.info.med.yale.edu/chldstudy/parentsfirst

[*Note*: Information regarding websites and addresses was accurate at the time of going to press. Neither the publishers nor the author can be responsible for any changes in website addresses or their content.]

Permissions

Short quotes from *Failure is not an Option* by Gene Kranz, Copyright ©
2000 by Gene Kranz. Reprinted permission of Simon and Schuster Adult
Publishing Group; short extract from *The Art of Thought* by Graham
Wallas. Copyright © 1926 by Harcourt Inc, and Mary Graham Wallas,
reprinted by permission of the publisher. Graham Wallas (1858–1932);
three Egyptian Hieroglyphs from *Introducing Egyptian Hieroglyphs* by
Barbara Watterson, published by Scottish Academic Press 1981, 1987.
Copyright © Barbara Watterson. Reprinted with kind permission of
author; item A5 from *Ravens Progressive Matrices* published by Oxford
Psychologists Press Limited. Reprinted with the kind permission of J.C.
Raven Limited, copyright© and Campbell Thompson & McLaughlin
Limited, Author's Agents; short quote from Albert Einstein with kind per-
mission of the *Albert Einstein Archives, the Hebrew University, Jerusalem.*

Index

Make
www.thorsonselement.com
your online sanctuary

Get online information, inspiration and
guidance to help you on the path to physical
and spiritual well-being. Drawing on the integrity
and vision of our authors and titles, and with
health advice, articles, astrology, tarot, a
meditation zone, author interviews and events
listings, www.thorsonselement.com is a great
alternative to help create space and peace
in our lives.

So if you've always wondered about practising
yoga, following an allergy-free diet, using the
tarot or getting a life coach, we can point you
in the right direction.

thorsons
element